Veloce *Classic Reprint* Series

The Collector's Guide

DIECAST TOY CARS

of the 1950s & 1960s

More from Veloce Publishing –

1½-litre GP Racing 1961-1965 (Whitelock)
AC Two-litre Saloons & Buckland Sportscars (Archibald)
Alfa Romeo 155/156/147 Competition Touring Cars (Collins)
Alfa Romeo Giulia Coupé GT & GTA (Tipler)
Alfa Romeo Montreal – The dream car that came true (Taylor)
Alfa Romeo Montreal – The Essential Companion (Classic Reprint of 500 copies) (Taylor)
Alfa Tipo 33 (McDonough & Collins)
Alpine & Renault – The Development of the Revolutionary Turbo F1 Car 1968 to 1979 (Smith)
Alpine & Renault – The Sports Prototypes 1963 to 1969 (Smith)
Alpine & Renault – The Sports Prototypes 1973 to 1978 (Smith)
Anatomy of the Classic Mini (Huthert & Ely)
Anatomy of the Works Minis (Moylan)
Armstrong-Siddeley (Smith)
Art Deco and British Car Design (Down)
Autodrome (Collins & Ireland)
Autodrome 2 (Collins & Ireland)
Automotive A-Z, Lane's Dictionary of Automotive Terms (Lane)
Automotive Mascots (Kay & Springate)
Bahamas Speed Weeks, The (O'Neil)
Bentley Continental, Corniche and Azure (Bennett)
Bentley MkVI, Rolls-Royce Silver Wraith, Dawn & Cloud/Bentley R & S-Series (Nutland)
Bluebird CN7 (Stevens)
BMC Competitions Department Secrets (Turner, Chambers & Browning)
BMW 5-Series (Cranswick)
BMW Z-Cars (Taylor)
BMW Boxer Twins 1970-1995 Bible, The (Falloon)
BMW Cafe Racers (Cloesen)
BMW Custom Motorcycles – Choppers, Cruisers, Bobbers, Trikes & Quads (Cloesen)
BMW – The Power of M (Vivian)
Bonjour – Is this Italy? (Turner)
British 250cc Racing Motorcycles (Pereira)
British at Indianapolis, The (Wagstaff)
British Cafe Racers (Cloesen)
British Cars, The Complete Catalogue of, 1895-1975 (Culshaw & Horrobin)
British Custom Motorcycles – The Brit Chop – choppers, cruisers, bobbers & trikes (Cloesen)
BRM – A Mechanic's Tale (Salmon)
BRM V16 (Ludvigsen)
BSA Bantam Bible, The (Henshaw)
BSA Motorcycles – the final evolution (Jones)
Bugatti Type 40 (Price)
Bugatti 46/50 Updated Edition (Price & Arbey)
Bugatti T44 & T49 (Price & Arbey)
Bugatti 57 2nd Edition (Price)
Bugatti Type 57 Grand Prix – A Celebration (Tomlinson)
Caravan, Improve & Modify Your (Porter)
Caravans, The Illustrated History 1919-1959 (Jenkinson)
Caravans, The Illustrated History From 1960 (Jenkinson)
Carrera Panamericana, La (Tipler)
Car-tastrophes – 80 automotive atrocities from the past 20 years (Honest John, Fowler)
Chrysler 300 – America's Most Powerful Car 2nd Edition (Ackerson)
Chrysler PT Cruiser (Ackerson)
Citroën DS (Bobbitt)
Classic British Car Electrical Systems (Astley)
Cobra – The Real Thing! (Legate)
Competition Car Aerodynamics 3rd Edition (McBeath)
Competition Car Composites A Practical Handbook (Revised 2nd Edition) (McBeath)
Concept Cars, How to illustrate and design (Dewey)
Cortina – Ford's Bestseller (Robson)
Cosworth - The Search for Power (6th edition) (Robson)
Coventry Climax Racing Engines (Hammill)
Daily Mirror 1970 World Cup Rally 40, The (Robson)
Daimler SP250 New Edition (Long)
Datsun Fairlady Roadster to 280ZX – The Z-Car Story (Long)
Dino – The V6 Ferrari (Long)
Dodge Challenger & Plymouth Barracuda (Grist)
Dodge Charger – Enduring Thunder (Ackerson)
Dodge Dynamite! (Grist)
Dorset from the Sea – The Jurassic Coast from Lyme Regis to Old Harry Rocks photographed from its best viewpoint (also Souvenir Edition) (Belasco)
Draw & Paint Cars – How to (Gardiner)
Drive on the Wild Side, A – 20 Extreme Driving Adventures From Around the World (Weaver)
Ducati 750 Bible, The (Falloon)
Ducati 750 SS 'round-case' 1974, The Book of the (Falloon)
Ducati 860, 900 and Mille Bible, The (Falloon)
Ducati Monster Bible (New Updated & Revised Edition), The (Falloon)
Ducati 916 (updated edition) (Falloon)
Dune Buggy, Building A – The Essential Manual (Shakespeare)
Dune Buggy Files (Hale)
Dune Buggy Handbook (Hale)
East German Motor Vehicles in Pictures (Suhr/Weinreich)
Fast Ladies – Female Racing Drivers 1888 to 1970 (Bouzanquet)
Fate of the Sleeping Beauties, The (op de Weegh/Hottendorff/op de Weegh)
Ferrari 288 GTO, The Book of the (Sackey)
Ferrari 333 SP (O'Neil)
Fiat & Abarth 124 Spider & Coupé (Tipler)
Fiat & Abarth 500 & 600 – 2nd Edition (Bobbitt)
Fiats, Great Small (Ward)
Fine Art of the Motorcycle Engine, The (Peirce)
Ford Cleveland 335-Series V8 engine 1970 to 1982 – The Essential Source Book (Hammill)
Ford F100/F150 Pick-up 1948-1996 (Ackerson)
Ford F150 Pick-up 1997-2005 (Ackerson)
Ford GT – Then, and Now (Streather)
Ford GT40 (Legate)
Ford Midsize Muscle – Fairlane, Torino & Ranchero (Cranswick)
Ford Model Y (Roberts)
Ford Small Block V8 Racing Engines 1962-1970 – The Essential Source Book (Hammill)
Ford Thunderbird From 1954, The Book of the (Long)
Formula 5000 Motor Racing, Back then ... and back now (Lawson)
Forza Minardi! (Vigar)
France: the essential guide for car enthusiasts – 200 things for the car enthusiast to see and do (Parish)
From Crystal Palace to Red Square – A Hapless Biker's Road to Russia (Turner)
Funky Mopeds (Skelton)
Grand Prix Ferrari – The Years of Enzo Ferrari's Power, 1948-1980 (Pritchard)
Grand Prix Ford – DFV-powered Formula 1 Cars (Robson)
GT – The World's Best GT Cars 1953-73 (Dawson)
Hillclimbing & Sprinting – The Essential Manual (Short & Wilkinson)
Honda NSX (Long)
Inside the Rolls-Royce & Bentley Styling Department – 1971 to 2001 (Hull)
Intermeccanica – The Story of the Prancing Bull (McCredie & Reisner)
Italian Cafe Racers (Cloesen)
Italian Custom Motorcycles (Cloesen)
Jaguar, The Rise of (Price)
Jaguar XJ 220 – The Inside Story (Moreton)
Jaguar XJ-S, The Book of the (Long)
Japanese Custom Motorcycles – The Nippon Chop – Chopper, Cruiser, Bobber, Trikes and Quads (Cloesen)
Jeep CJ (Ackerson)
Jeep Wrangler (Ackerson)
The Jowett Jupiter - The car that leaped to fame (Nankivell)
Karmann-Ghia Coupé & Convertible (Bobbitt)
Kawasaki Triples Bible, The (Walker)
Kawasaki Z1 Story, The (Sheehan)
Kris Meeke – Intercontinental Rally Challenge Champion (McBride)
Lamborghini Miura Bible, The (Sackey)
Lamborghini Urraco, The Book of the (Landsem)
Lambretta Bible, The (Davies)
Lancia 037 (Collins)
Lancia Delta HF Integrale (Blaettel & Wagner)
Land Rover Series III Reborn (Porter)
Land Rover, The Half-ton Military (Cook)
Laverda Twins & Triples Bible 1968-1986 (Falloon)
Lea-Francis Story, The (Price)
Le Mans Panoramic (Ireland)
Lexus Story, The (Long)
Little book of microcars, the (Quellin)
Little book of smart, the – New Edition (Jackson)
Little book of trikes, the (Quellin)
Lola – The Illustrated History (1957-1977) (Starkey)
Lola – All the Sports Racing & Single-seater Racing Cars 1978-1997 (Starkey)
Lola T70 – The Racing History & Individual Chassis Record – 4th Edition (Starkey)
Lotus 18 Colin Chapman's U-turn (Whitelock)
Lotus 49 (Oliver)
Marketingmobiles, The Wonderful Wacky World of (Hale)
Maserati 250F In Focus (Pritchard)
Mazda MX-5/Miata 1.6 Enthusiast's Workshop Manual (Grainger & Shoemark)
Mazda MX-5/Miata 1.8 Enthusiast's Workshop Manual (Grainger & Shoemark)
Mazda MX-5 Miata, The book of the – The 'Mk1' NA-series 1988 to 1997 (Long)
Mazda MX-5 Miata Roadster (Long)
Mazda Rotary-engined Cars (Cranswick)
Maximum Mini (Booij)
Meet the English (Bowie)
Mercedes-Benz SL – R230 series 2001 to 2011 (Long)
Mercedes-Benz SL – W113-series 1963-1971 (Long)
Mercedes-Benz SL & SLC – 107-series 1971-1989 (Long)
Mercedes-Benz SLK – R170 series 1996-2004 (Long)
Mercedes-Benz SLK – R171 series 2004-2011 (Long)
Mercedes-Benz W123-series – All models 1976 to 1986 (Long)
Mercedes G-Wagen (Long)
MGA (Price Williams)
MGB & MGB GT– Expert Guide (Auto-doc Series) (Williams)
MGB Electrical Systems Updated & Revised Edition (Astley)
Micro Caravans (Jenkinson)
Micro Trucks (Mort)
Microcars at Large! (Quellin)
Mini Cooper – The Real Thing! (Tipler)
Mini Minor to Asia Minor (West)
Mitsubishi Lancer Evo, The Road Car & WRC Story (Long)
Montlhéry, The Story of the Paris Autodrome (Boddy)
Morgan Maverick (Lawrence)
Morgan 3 Wheeler – back to the future!, The (Dron)
Morris Minor, 60 Years on the Road (Newell)
Moto Guzzi Sport & Le Mans Bible, The (Falloon)
Motor Movies – The Posters! (Veysey)
Motor Racing – Reflections of a Lost Era (Carter)
Motor Racing – The Pursuit of Victory 1930-1962 (Carter)
Motor Racing – The Pursuit of Victory 1963-1972 (Wyatt/Sears)
Motor Racing Heroes – The Stories of 100 Greats (Newman)
Motorcycle Apprentice (Cakebread)
Motorcycle GP Racing in the 1960s (Pereira)
Motorcycle Road & Racing Chassis Designs (Noakes)
Motorhomes, The Illustrated History (Jenkinson)
Motorsport In colour, 1950s (Wainwright)
MV Agusta Fours, The book of the classic (Falloon)
N.A.R.T. – A concise history of the North American Racing Team 1957 to 1983 (O'Neil)
Nissan 300ZX & 350Z – The Z-Car Story (Long)
Nissan GT-R Supercar: Born to race (Gorodji)
Northeast American Sports Car Races 1950-1959 (O'Neil)
The Norton Commando Bible – All models 1968 to 1978 (Henshaw)
Nothing Runs – Misadventures in the Classic, Collectable & Exotic Car Biz (Slutsky)
Off-Road Giants! (Volume 1) – Heroes of 1960s Motorcycle Sport (Westlake)
Off-Road Giants! (Volume 2) – Heroes of 1960s Motorcycle Sport (Westlake)
Off-Road Giants! (volume 3) – Heroes of 1960s Motorcycle Sport (Westlake)
Pass the Theory and Practical Driving Tests (Gibson & Hoole)
Peking to Paris 2007 (Young)
Pontiac Firebird – New 3rd Edition (Cranswick)
Porsche Boxster (Long)
Porsche 356 (2nd Edition) (Long)
Porsche 908 (Födisch, Neßhöver, Roßbach, Schwarz & Roßbach)
Porsche 911 Carrera – The Last of the Evolution (Corlett)
Porsche 911R, RS & RSR, 4th Edition (Starkey)
Porsche 911, The Book of the (Long)
Porsche 911 – The Definitive History 2004-2012 (Long)
Porsche – The Racing 914s (Smith)
Porsche 911SC 'Super Carrera' – The Essential Companion (Streather)
Porsche 914 & 914-6: The Definitive History of the Road & Competition Cars (Long)
Porsche 924 (Long)
The Porsche 924 Carreras – evolution to excellence (Smith)
Porsche 928 (Long)
Porsche 944 (Long)
Porsche 964, 993 & 996 Data Plate Code Breaker (Streather)
Porsche 993 'King Of Porsche' – The Essential Companion (Streather)
Porsche 996 'Supreme Porsche' – The Essential Companion (Streather)
Porsche 997 2004-2012 – Porsche Excellence (Streather)
Porsche Racing Cars – 1953 to 1975 (Long)
Porsche Racing Cars – 1976 to 2005 (Long)
Porsche – The Rally Story (Meredith)
Porsche: Three Generations of Genius (Meredith)
Preston Tucker & Others (Linde)
RAC Rally Action! (Gardiner)
RACING COLOURS – MOTOR RACING COMPOSITIONS 1908-2009 (Newman)
Racing Line – British motorcycle racing in the golden age of the big single (Guntrip)
Rallye Sport Fords: The Inside Story (Moreton)
Renewable Energy Home Handbook, The (Porter)
Roads with a View – England's greatest views and how to find them by road (Corfield)
Rolls-Royce Silver Shadow/Bentley T Series Corniche & Camargue – Revised & Enlarged Edition (Bobbitt)
Rolls-Royce Silver Spirit, Silver Spur & Bentley Mulsanne 2nd Edition (Bobbitt)
Rootes Cars of the 50s, 60s & 70s – Hillman, Humber, Singer, Sunbeam & Talbot (Rowe)
Rover P4 (Bobbitt)
Runways & Racers (O'Neil)
Russian Motor Vehicles – Soviet Limousines 1930-2003 (Kelly)
Russian Motor Vehicles – The Czarist Period 1784 to 1917 (Kelly)
RX-7 – Mazda's Rotary Engine Sports car (Updated & Revised New Edition) (Long)
Scooters & Microcars, The A-Z of Popular (Dan)
Scooter Lifestyle (Grainger)
SCOOTER MANIA! – Recollections of the Isle of Man International Scooter Rally (Jackson)
Singer Story: Cars, Commercial Vehicles, Bicycles & Motorcycle (Atkinson)
Sleeping Beauties USA – abandoned classic cars & trucks (Marek)
SM – Citroën's Maserati-engined Supercar (Long & Claverol)
Speedway – Auto racing's ghost tracks (Collins & Ireland)
Sprite Caravans, The Story of (Jenkinson)
Standard Motor Company, The Book of the (Robson)
Steve Hole's Kit Car Cornucopia – Cars, Companies, Stories, Facts & Figures: the UK's kit car scene since 1949 (Hole)
Subaru Impreza: The Road Car And WRC Story (Long)
Supercar, How to Build your own (Thompson)
Tales from the Toolbox (Oliver)
Tatra – The Legacy of Hans Ledwinka, Updated & Enlarged Collector's Edition of 1500 copies (Margolius & Henry)
Taxi! The Story of the 'London' Taxicab (Bobbitt)
To Boldly Go – twenty six vehicle designs that dared to be different (Hull)
Toleman Story, The (Hilton)
Toyota Celica & Supra, The Book of Toyota's Sports Coupés (Long)
Toyota MR2 Coupés & Spyders (Long)
Triumph Bonneville Bible (59-83) (Henshaw)
Triumph Bonneville!, Save the – The inside story of the Meriden Workers' Co-op (Rosamond)
Triumph Motorcycles & the Meriden Factory (Hancox)
Triumph Speed Twin & Thunderbird Bible (Woolridge)
Triumph Tiger Cub Bible (Estall)
Triumph Trophy Bible (Woolridge)
Triumph TR6 (Kimberley)
TT Talking – The TT's most exciting era – As seen by Manx Radio TT's lead commentator 2004-2012 (Lambert)
Two Summers – The Mercedes-Benz W196R Racing Car (Ackerson)
TWR Story, The – Group A (Hughes & Scott)
Unraced (Collins)
Velocette Motorcycles – MSS to Thruxton – New Third Edition (Burris)
Vespa – The Story of a Cult Classic in Pictures (Uhlig)
Vincent Motorcycles: The Untold Story since 1946 (Guyony & Parker)
Volkswagen Bus Book, The (Bobbitt)
Volkswagen Bus or Van to Camper, How to Convert (Porter)
Volkswagens of the World (Glen)
VW Beetle Cabriolet – The full story of the convertible Beetle (Bobbitt)
VW Beetle – The Car of the 20th Century (Copping)
VW Bus – 40 Years of Splitties, Bays & Wedges (Copping)
VW Bus Book, The (Bobbitt)
VW Golf: Five Generations of Fun (Copping & Cservenka)
VW – The Air-cooled Era (Copping)
VW T5 Camper Conversion Manual (Porter)
VW Campers (Copping)
Volkswagen Type 3, The book of the – Concept, Design, International Production Models & Development (Glen)
You & Your Jaguar XK8/XKR – Buying, Enjoying, Maintaining, Modifying – New Edition (Thorley)
Which Oil? – Choosing the right oils & greases for your antique, vintage, veteran, classic or collector car (Michell)
Works Minis, The Last (Purves & Brenchley)
Works Rally Mechanic (Moylan)

www.velocebooks.com

First published in April 2009, this edition printed June 2017 by Veloce Publishing Limited, Parkway Farm Business Park, Middle Farm Way, Poundbury, Dorchester DT1 3AR, England. Fax 01305 250479 / e-mail info@veloce.co.uk / web www.veloce.co.uk or www.velocebooks.com.
ISBN: 978-1-787111-17-2/UPC: 6-36847-01117-8
© Andrew Ralston and Veloce Publishing 2009 & 2017. All rights reserved. With the exception of quoting brief passages for the purpose of review, no part of this publication may be recorded, reproduced or transmitted by any means, including photocopying, without the written permission of Veloce Publishing Ltd. Throughout this book logos, model names and designations, etc, have been used for the purposes of identification, illustration and decoration. Such names are the property of the trademark holder as this is not an official publication. Note that Mattel makes no representation as to the authenticity of the materials obtained herein. The author assumes full responsibility for facts and information contained in this book. All opinions expressed are those of the author's and not of Mattel Inc.
Readers with ideas for automotive books, or books on other transport or related hobby subjects, are invited to write to the editorial director of Veloce Publishing at the above address.
British Library Cataloguing in Publication Data - A catalogue record for this book is available from the British Library. Typesetting, design and page make-up all by Veloce Publishing Ltd on Apple Mac.
Printed and Bound by CPI Group (UK) Ltd, Croydon, CR04YY.

Veloce *Classic Reprint* Series

DIECAST TOY CARS

The Collector's Guide

of the 1950s & 1960s

DYNA JUNIOR

DINKY TOYS
102
M.G. MIDGET SPORTS MADE IN N.IRELAND

SPOT-ON
...dels by Tri-ang
Regd. Trade Mark

Dinky, Corgi and Spot-On, Solido and CIJ, Märklin and Gama,
Tekno and Mercury, Diapet and Cherryca Phenix

Andrew Ralston

CONTENTS

INTRODUCTION

Anyone who was a child in the 1950s or 1960s will recall with a nostalgic glow the days when toy shop windows were full of brightly coloured Dinky Toys' miniatures sitting on top of their yellow boxes, and how the weekly pocket money allowance would just about stretch to the purchase of a model of the family Triumph Herald or Ford Anglia.

Even in today's computerized world toy cars still have an irresistible appeal for many youngsters, as the success of the Disney film *Cars* and all its spin-off merchandise proves, while the diecast toy industry has gained a further lease of life by catering for an entirely different clientele: adult collectors. In fact, there are probably more diecast models of classic cars of the 1950s-1970s in production today than there were at the time!

This book does not try to provide a comprehensive guide to every toy car ever made. The closest thing to a definitive catalogue is the Italian collector Paolo Rampini's monumental *Golden Book of Model Cars 1900-1975* which lists some 25,000 items.

Nor is this the kind of book that provides minute descriptions of colour variations, different types of wheels or introduction and deletion dates of every model. Detailed information of that kind is already available in the many excellent specialist one-make histories of companies such as Dinky Toys, Corgi Toys and Matchbox listed in the bibliography on page 123.

Instead, the present volume gives a broad overview of the development of diecast toy car production in Britain, mainland Europe, the USA, and beyond. Most of the major brands are

Children playing with Dinky Toys cars and trucks on the living room floor. This 1957 photograph sums up the nostalgic appeal of toy cars – perhaps the most powerful motivation behind the adult collecting hobby today.

covered, but particular attention is given to providing background information on the more obscure manufacturers.

While these manufacturers are looked at individually, the links between them are also stressed. For example, some brands emerged in direct competition with more established ones. Sometimes a good idea was copied by others. Sometimes the success of a newcomer posed a threat – as in the case of the late 1960s Hot Wheels phenomenon from America, which forced Matchbox, Lone Star and others to develop similar types of models. Thereafter, toy cars became increasingly 'gimmicky': children expected them 'to do things' rather than simply to be representations of a particular vehicle. For this reason, most collectors consider the 1950s and 1960s to be the classic era of the diecast toy car and the models pictured here are, therefore, drawn from this period.

With so many thousands to choose from, it has inevitably been necessary to be very selective in deciding which models to show. A representative selection of models by the major brands such as Dinky and Corgi has been included, but the bias in the illustrations is towards the more unusual items, many of which have not been pictured in any other publication. Where possible, at least one example of the products of each manufacturer has been included.

This book would not have been possible without the enthusiastic participation of some of the world's most prominent collectors who kindly contributed photographs. Special thanks are due to the following: Bruce Sterling (USA), who is well-known for possessing what is possibly the world's finest collection of mint and boxed Japanese toy cars; Gary Cohen (USA), who owns many scarce items from the UK, Israel and Argentina; Douglas R. Kelly (USA), author of *The Die Cast Price Guide*; Alex J. Cameron (Scotland); Juan Mauri Cruz (Spain); David Ralston (Scotland).

A QUESTION OF SCALE

The typical diecast toy car is usually described as being to 1/43 scale – a size which was adopted to fit in with 'O' gauge model railways. In reality, though, few 1950s-60s diecasts were consistent in this respect, a notable exception being Tri-ang's Spot-On range where every item was to 1/42 scale. Many Dinky and Corgi models varied between 1/40 and 1/50, while the advent of the Matchbox series in 1953 created a new market for 1/72-1/90 models.

Unless otherwise stated, models pictured are around 1/40-1/50 scale. The occasional larger item is referred to by its length.

A NOTE ON VALUATIONS

Each model pictured in this book is accompanied by an indication of its current value. In some cases a price range (e.g. £100-£150) is quoted. The colour of the model, for example, might determine whether the item achieves a price at the upper or lower end of the range. The key factor in all cases is condition, and it's important to realise that these prices refer only to items in mint condition, with boxes that are clean and complete. A played-with toy with chipped paintwork without the original box, or in a box that is damaged, will be worth much less.

Models by major manufacturers appear regularly on internet sales or at specialist auctions run by Vectis Auctions and others. As such, it's possible to establish a 'going rate' for such items. The prices quoted for Dinky, Corgi, Matchbox, Budgie, Spot-On and French Dinky models are based on the 2008 edition of the price guide published by *Model Collector* magazine which has been used with the kind permission of the editor, Lindsey Amrani. The price guide may be obtained via the magazine's website www.modelcollector.co.uk.

In the case of other brands of diecast toys exact values are harder to establish. When examples of a toy rarely appear on the market, prices can vary widely. Collectors competing to acquire a particularly rare piece can push the price well above what the seller was expecting. However, the prices quoted will at least give some indication of the relative rarity of one model compared to another. Thus, if the suggested value for an item pictured in this book is £200 while another is quoted at £50, it is safe to say that the first will be harder to find. On the other hand, that does not mean that when an example of the toy comes up for sale it will definitely sell for £200. The difficulty of establishing exact values for unusual toys can easily be seen by studying auction and eBay results: sometimes a reserve price will not be reached, whereas on other occasions the toy can sell for three or four times the price expected!

In France in the mid-1950s this offer on packets of coffee allowed the purchaser to claim a free Dinky Toys car.

For many years one brand had a virtual monopoly of the British diecast toy market: Dinky. Even today – nearly thirty years since the last Dinky car left the Meccano factory in Liverpool – there are still plenty of people who refer to any miniature vehicle as a 'Dinky toy' in much the same way that they call any vacuum cleaner a 'Hoover.'

The man behind the Dinky range was Frank Hornby (1863-1936), a former employee of a Liverpool meat import company, someone with a fertile imagination and many interests: singing, temperance work, and, above all, engineering and mechanics. Hornby spent his spare time making mechanical gadgets for his two sons, Roland and Douglas, to play with, and these eventually bore fruit in a construction toy that went on sale in 1902 as 'Mechanics Made Easy' – better known as Meccano from 1907 onwards. Hornby, who was to gain fame as 'the man who made a million with a toy,' originally had to borrow £5 from his employer to begin production. Meccano was followed by Hornby clockwork trains, and trains needed accessories to make them more realistic ... hence the appearance in 1933 of a set of six vehicles priced at four shillings, containing a tank, tractor, van, truck and two cars, initially sold as 'Modelled Miniatures' and subsequently as Dinky Toys. Mike Richardson, author of *The Great Book of Dinky Toys*, dates the first use of the Dinky name to April 1934.

Dinky Toys

From these modest beginnings, a vast range of models developed. Just six years later the Dinky range contained as many as "250 charming varieties" – not just cars, trucks and buses, but also aircraft, model ships and accessories like figures, petrol pumps and garages. Toy manufacture more or less ceased during the war years, though a notable exception was the production of a miniature Spitfire fighter aircraft which was sold in order to raise money to fund a real one. After the war, Dinky – just like the real car manufacturers – reintroduced prewar models, but new subjects were quickly added, the first two being a Lagonda sports and a US Army Jeep, described as 'a wonderfully realistic miniature of the most famous car of the war.' Many new postwar cars followed, including the Austin A40 Devon, Jaguar XK 120, Standard Vanguard, Rover 75 and Ford Zephyr.

Children were eager to have new Dinky Toys after World War II. This 1946 advertisement shows the first two postwar releases: a Lagonda sports and a US Army Jeep.

Dinky's position as brand leader was unchallenged in the first half of the 1950s and sales continued to grow. Britain emerged from the difficult days of postwar austerity and entered the period of prosperity famously summed up in Prime Minister Harold Macmillan's reputed comment to voters: "You've never had it so good." The 'feelgood factor' was reflected in the greater availability and affordability of toys for children.

The Dinky range grew in size but the basic concept did not change: the cars had simple one-piece body castings fitted to tinplate bases, with only the larger and more expensive lorries having operating features like opening doors, winding cranes, and extending ladders. This was the era of the Foden and Leyland eight-wheel trucks (sold under the 'Dinky Supertoys' name), the Guy Vans with colourful liveries like 'Weetabix' and 'Golden Shred,' plus the series of British sports cars like the Austin-Healey, MG Midget and Sunbeam Alpine.

The Dinky Toys Club

The Meccano Company launched a club for collectors of Dinky Toys in January 1957 (Corgi had already set up such a club the previous year). Members received a certificate signed by Club President Roland Hornby, an enamel badge, and a collector's licence in a format similar to a driving licence. In addition, a regular newsletter was sent out to members informing them of new releases, supplementing the *Dinky Toy News* articles published monthly in Meccano's in-house journal, the *Meccano Magazine,* which in 1962 had a monthly circulation of about 75,000. Stirling Moss, the most famous racing driver of the day, was the holder of Licence No.1 and each month ten club members were selected at random to receive their choice of Dinky Toys' models to the value of £2 sterling – which, at that time, would buy up to ten models. The club doesn't seem to have lasted beyond 1963.

The market extended far beyond the British Isles. Even before the war Meccano had catered for the lucrative American market with the 39 Series of six American cars: Packard Super 8, Oldsmobile 6, Lincoln Zephyr, Buick Viceroy, Chrysler Royal, and Studebaker State Commander. During the fifties Dinky brought out many of the tail-finned American cars like the Dodge Royal, De Soto Fireflite, Studebaker President and Packard Clipper – cars that would have looked very exotic to British children. Meccano had an agent in New York, H Hudson Dobson Inc., which handled North American sales.

In 1961 38 per cent of the company's production was exported to over forty different countries, and many separate editions of the annual Dinky catalogue were printed for export markets all round the world. Dinky toys even found their way behind the Iron Curtain. In 1961 the Soviet leader Nikita Kruschev visited Meccano Limited's display at the British Trade Fair in Moscow and described it as "a children's paradise." According to Meccano's Export Manager, Norman Craig, 150,000 catalogues were given away at the exhibition. The following year, at a Trade Fair in Romania, Leyland Motors had a display of Dinky Leyland trucks to give visitors an impression of what the actual vehicles looked like.

However, with success came complacency. 'More of the same' seemed an infallible recipe and Meccano had no difficulty in selling everything it made. As a result, the company did not appreciate the threat when serious competitors began to emerge.

Matchbox

At the end of the Second World War, Rodney Smith and Leslie Smith – two ex-servicemen who shared the same surname but were not

This 1958 Meccano Limited catalogue is typical of the type of artwork used in the company's publicity material, showing an excited schoolboy with a selection of Dinky Toys models, Hornby trains and Meccano.

An original store display for the American market, showing the full Matchbox 1-75 range for 1960. (Courtesy Gary Cohen)

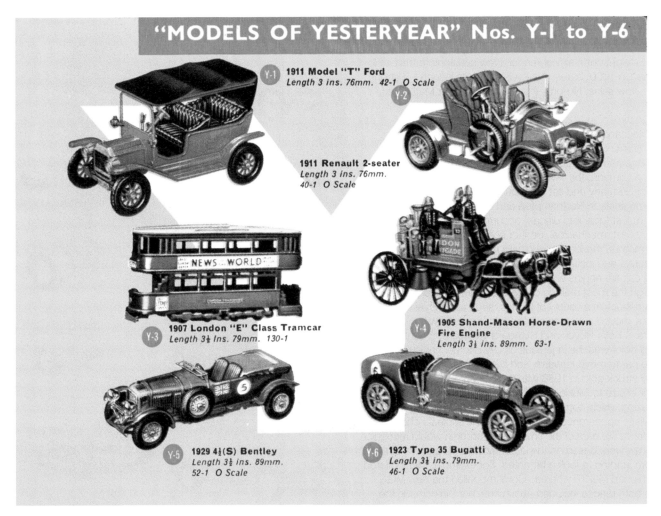

Y-1 1911 Model "T" Ford
Length 3 ins. 76mm. 42-1 O Scale

Y-2 1911 Renault 2-seater
Length 3 ins. 76mm.
40-1 O Scale

Y-3 1907 London "E" Class Tramcar
Length 3⅛ ins. 79mm. 130-1

Y-4 1905 Shand-Mason Horse-Drawn
Fire Engine
Length 3½ ins. 89mm. 63-1

Y-5 1929 4½(S) Bentley
Length 3½ ins. 89mm.
52-1 O Scale

Y-6 1923 Type 35 Bugatti
Length 3⅛ ins. 79mm.
46-1 O Scale

Another Lesney innovation was the 'Models of Yesteryear' series. Many manufacturers followed in Lesney's footsteps with models of vintage cars.

related – decided to set up in business. They put their war gratuities of £300 together to purchase a diecasting machine and came up with a name for their company, Lesney, simply by combining letters from their first names. They were later joined by Jack Odell, a skilled engineer.

At first Lesney manufactured industrial components, but in a slack period Odell made some moulds and started producing diecast vehicles which sold well. Lesney's big breakthrough, however, was a model of the Coronation Coach, over one million of which were sold as a souvenir of the Coronation of Queen Elizabeth II in 1953. This led Jack Odell to envisage a series of miniature diecast models, the first example being a small road roller which he made for his daughter who took it to school inside an empty matchbox.

From this brainwave developed the Matchbox series, cheap enough for children to buy with their pocket money. After a lukewarm response from the toy trade, these small toys rapidly grew in popularity from 1954 onwards and soon the series had expanded to 75 models. Jack Odell's next inspired idea was the 1956 'Yesteryear' series of vintage cars and trucks, which also included a traction engine and a tram. Small-scale toy cars and models of vintage vehicles had a profound influence on the diecast market, and many other companies in Britain and beyond imitated Matchbox products – sometimes quite openly. In 1960 shares in Lesney Products were offered for sale, and by 1966 the company was employing 3600 people and making 100 million models a year. Lesney continued to go from strength to strength, winning the Queen's Award to Industry in 1966, 1968 and 1969.

While small Matchbox cars were not directly competing against the larger Dinky Toys products, they clearly encroached on Meccano's share of the market. Dinky responded in 1957 with its own small scale cars, Dublo Dinky Toys, named after Hornby-Dublo railways for which they were marketed as accessories. Most of the Dublo models were small commercial vehicles of the type that might be seen in and around railway stations. Two cars – a Ford Prefect and Singer roadster – and an Austin taxi were introduced in 1959, a year before Matchbox brought out a similar model. New additions to the Dublo range ceased in 1960, barely three years after its launch – a strong indicator of slow sales. No-one, it seems, could beat Matchbox!

Corgi Toys

However, Meccano Ltd faced still more competition when a newcomer challenged Dinky head-on in 1956: Corgi Toys. The maker, Mettoy, had been active in the UK toy market since 1933 when Philipp Ullmann, the owner of the German company Tipp and Co fled Nazi Germany and set up in business making tinplate and other toys, originally in Northampton and later in Swansea.

Mettoy's first foray into diecast occurred in 1948 with the launch of six 'heavy cast, mechanical, perfect scale models.' Powered by clockwork motors, these were originally made for sale in Marks and Spencer stores, and included a coach, articulated truck, delivery van, racing car, fire engine and saloon car. These only lasted a few years, though the most realistic of them, a Morris delivery van, later made a comeback in a variety of liveries, such as a Royal Mail van. Next, Mettoy moved a step closer to Dinky's ground with two smaller diecast cars, a Rolls-Royce and Standard Vanguard, though the main selling point was the ingenious clockwork mechanism which allowed the car to move forwards and backwards.

Mettoy struck gold in 1956 with the launch of Corgi. Corgi toys were similar in size to Dinkies, but had the extra refinement of plastic window glazing which, together with spun metal wheels, gave them a more realistic appearance. As with Dinky, the subjects chosen were popular family cars of the time that all children would recognise, but the Corgis were based on the latest models while some of the Dinkies were starting to look a bit dated. For example, Dinky offered the old-fashioned MG TF whereas Corgi modelled the new MGA sports car; both ranges included Austin cars but Dinky made the Devon and Somerset while Corgi had the latest Cambridge.

Furthermore, the arrival of Corgi was warmly welcomed by the toy trade: some shops found it hard to get supplies of Dinky toys as Meccano Limited didn't encourage new retailers to stock its toys, as it already had wide market coverage. Corgi, by contrast, took a proactive approach and soon the new range was appearing in toy shops all over the country.

At first Dinky's only response was to brighten up some of its cars by issuing them in what were described as 'gay two-tone colours.' It wasn't until 1958 that a Dinky car appeared with window glazing, the Austin A105. From then on the company tended to lag behind Corgi in the race to be first to fit more and more gimmicks – opening doors, bonnets, boots, suspension, steering, and so on.

Nevertheless, Dinky toys were still good sellers. Roland Hornby's report to shareholders in 1956 referred to "increased competition abroad and a more difficult home market," but even as late as 1963 a 20,000 square foot extension was being added to Meccano's Binns Road factory in Liverpool to allow Dinky production to be stepped up to half a million toys per week.

The Corgi range began in 1956 and had expanded significantly by 1960. This selection of sports and racing cars was shown in the catalogue for that year.

Spot-On

Yet another diecast range was launched in 1959: Spot-On, from the Tri-ang company owned by Lines Brothers, who had long been famous for large toys like pedal cars, and whose plastic Tri-ang railways had already seriously hit sales of Meccano's Hornby-Dublo range. Lines Brothers liked to operate on a big scale: in 1959 they owned twenty factories in Britain, Ireland, New Zealand, Canada, Australia and France.

Tri-ang's entry into the diecast market was typically ambitious. Company Chairman Walter Lines enthusiastically announced to shareholders at the Annual General Meeting in 1959 that "Spot-On Models Ltd. had been formed to make a complete range of miniature road transport vehicles and cars, all in exact 1/42 scale." 'Complete range' meant just that: not only cars, trucks and buses, but "a complete flexible roadway system with all normal buildings ... to the same scale." The interlocking road sections were made of tinplate; the buildings were rubber mouldings, and plastic figures were available, too. Tri-ang's factory in Castlereagh Road, Belfast, had already been extended in order to produce the Spot-On range.

Hugely prized by collectors today, Spot-On never really caught on at the time: the scale of 1/42 made them look big and clumsy against Dinky and Corgi models; distribution to the toy trade was patchy, and they were considerably more expensive to buy than other model cars – partly as a result of the 'constant scale' policy, which the other manufacturers did not follow. For example, when Dinky or Corgi made a double deck bus, they scaled it down, whereas Spot-On's London Routemaster was the right size to go with the cars, but needed much more metal to make it. Spot-On struggled on until 1967, with limited production continuing thereafter in Lines Brothers' New Zealand factory.

By the time of Spot-On's demise, Corgi sales had rocketed ahead with the move into film-related toys, especially the phenomenally successful *James Bond* Aston Martin (1965), which came complete with ejector seat, retractable machine guns and revolving rear number plate. By the 1970s Corgi was employing 2500 people and producing sixty million vehicles a year. Corgi even tried to challenge Matchbox with a range of small scale models issued in 1964 under the Husky name and initially sold through branches of Woolworths. After 1969 they were renamed Corgi Juniors and distributed more widely.

Dinky struggled in vain to keep up. Some success was achieved with the Gerry Anderson *Thunderbirds* and *Captain Scarlet* models, but the company's underlying weakness could no longer be concealed. As Professor Kenneth D Brown puts it in *Factory of Dreams*, his authoritative history of Meccano Limited, the Binns Road factory was suffering from "a combination of mismanagement and complacency, the

The box of each early Spot-On model contained a picture of the vehicle inside. Members of the Spot-On collectors' club received an album to keep these in.

Corgi quickly followed up the massive success of the James Bond Aston Martin with similar toys. The Avengers and The Man from U.N.C.L.E were popular television series of the 1960s.

twin outcomes of easy long-term success and weak leadership."[1] Frank Hornby's son Roland, who ran the company from 1936 until 1964, was said to be more interested in the golf course than in the business!

Mounting losses led to a takeover by the other British toy giant, Lines Brothers, in 1964, inevitably hastening the end of Lines' own model car range, Spot-On. Once Lines ran into difficulties, Airfix took over. Managing Directors came and went but every attempt to improve the company's efficiency ended in failure. The inevitable announcement came in 1979: "The Board of Meccano Ltd. regrets to announce that the continuing and heavy losses of its factory at Binns Road have resulted in a decision to cease manufacture at the close of business on Friday, 30th November."

Minor brands

The story of these four big names in the history of British diecast toys – Dinky, Matchbox, Corgi and Spot-On – has been told in great detail, in definitive books and endless magazine articles listing and describing every model variation. Behind these well-known names, though, lies an 'alternative' British diecast story which, until recently, has received comparatively less attention – the story of numerous smaller brands that came and went without leaving much trace.[2]

During the Second World War toys, like other consumer goods, were in short supply; raw materials were not available for toy manufacture, and toy factories switched to the production of weapons, ammunition, and other wartime requirements. After six years of wartime shortages, there was a huge demand for new toys. By 1946 the ban on the use of metal for toy production was lifted, and only six months after V.E. Day Lines Brothers was back in full production, churning out tinplate Minic cars, Pedigree dolls, soft toys and outdoor toys like scooters and pedal cars.

This was a time when almost anything would sell, and for this reason many small toy companies flourished briefly, making rather crude and poorly-finished products. However, the Korean War of 1951 again led to a ban on the use of zinc for toymaking; thereafter, when better quality diecast toys like those from Dinky Toys and the Matchbox series became more widely available, many of the smaller brand names fell by the wayside. Neverthless, throughout the fifties, numerous established toy companies, large and small, attempted to break into the diecast car market.

The history of model car production in the UK would not be complete without reference to these fascinating minor players, and the remainder of this chapter provides a survey of some of the less familiar names in British diecast.

Timpo

A typical example would be the crude diecast cars sold under the Timpo name, which simply stands for 'Toy Importers Limited,' a company founded in 1938 by a Mr. Sally Gawrylowicz. As wartime conditions made importation impossible, Timpo started making its own toys, such as aeroplanes and figures, using a composition material as well as more traditional toy forts and garages made from wood.

Timpo was quick to bring out metal toy cars after the war. Play value was certainly high, as the cars were accompanied by accessories, such as petrol pumps, figures and garage buildings, but they were hardly scale models, with some barely resembling an identifiable prototype. The range could not compete against the much more realistic Dinky Toys' items, and production doesn't seem to have resumed after the 1951 metal ban. The Timpo name lived on, however, as a maker of metal soldiers, farm animals, and cowboy figures. In fact, Timpo was still making plastic figures as recently as 1979.[3]

Charbens

Brothers Charles and Benjamin Reid combined their first names to create Charbens in the 1920s, making mostly lead soldiers and farm animals. After the Second World War, Charbens produced numerous model lorries, vans, horse-drawn vehicles, and a bus, all of which were as crudely put together as the Timpos. In 1955 the 'Old Crocks' series of Matchbox-size veteran and vintage cars was launched, boxed in 'packing crate' style cardboard cartons. Unfortunately, the quality of metal used by Charbens was often poor, causing many examples to suffer from metal fatigue which causes cracks or even holes to form. Consequently, few of these toys survive in mint condition, though the 'Old Crocks' are still relatively common.

Benbros

Benbros was a similar type of company, founded in the late forties by brothers Jack and Nathan Benenson, hence the name 'Benbros.' Their main contribution was a series of Matchbox-inspired toys initially sold as the 'TV Series' on account of their boxes which were designed to look like television sets. These were launched in 1954, barely a year after the Matchbox originals, and lasted until about 1956 or 1957 when the name was changed to 'Mighty Midgets.' Benbros also made larger diecast tractors, military vehicles, motorcycles and trucks, with its AA Land Rover being the best of the series. In the early sixties quality improved with the short lived 'Zebra Toys.' Two models in this series, the Jaguar E Type Coupé and a Heinkel Bubble Car, are highly-prized on the collecting market today. Production ceased around 1965.

The River Series

Intially, the makers of the River Series, Jordan and Lewden Limited of Homerton, East London, were not directly involved in the toy industry but made industrial castings. The river in question was not the Thames but the River Jordan, chosen because of the name of one of the founders and also because the company had Jewish connections. At the January 1957 Toy Fair at Harrogate, Yorkshire, Jordan and Lewden exhibited "diecast cowboy pistols, cars, trucks, garage parts and souvenir lines."

[1] Kenneth D Brown, Factory of Dreams: A History of Meccano Ltd, p. 108 (quoted by permission of Crucible Books, Lancaster)
[2] www.lone-star-diecast-bk.com provides a comprehensive source of information on toys by DCMT Lone Star and www.robertnewson.co.uk contains detailed histories of many of the smaller postwar British diecast manufacturers.
[3] The history of Timpo diecast cars was traced in detail in articles by Robert Newson in Model Collector magazine, October/November 1988.

The River Series contained six cars: a Ford Prefect, Daimler Conquest, Buick, Standard Vanguard saloon and estate car, and an Austin Somerset, and these can be found with or without friction motors, some of them with a plated finish similar to that used on the toy guns. In addition, there were numerous commercial vehicles. The River Series toys were a little better than those from Timpo but nowhere near the standard of a Dinky or Corgi toy. Unboxed examples can be hard to identify as they are simply marked 'Made in England.'

The range faded away after a few years, but came to life again in a different form in Israel, where the dies were reused by Gamda (see page 109).

DCMT and Crescent

Like Jordan and Lewden, DCMT (Die Casting Machine Tools) was not initially a toy company. In 1940 A.R. Mills designed and built his own diecasting machine in a garage in Palmers Green, North London. With a partner, Sidney Ambridge, he set up DCMT to make similar machines. Inevitably, DCMT did business with toy companies that used their diecasting equipment – it was, in fact, a DCMT machine that the founders of Lesney purchased with their service gratuities in 1947. To illustrate the capabilities of its machinery, it was logical for DCMT to start making toys itself. Initially these were marketed by Crescent, the most successful being a Jaguar saloon car which was offered in various sets with figures or accessories and which is still quite easy to find today. Crescent, like Charbens, had been in existence since the 1920s making hollow cast metal soldiers and other figures. After 1950, DCMT and Crescent went their separate ways. Crescent moved to South Wales and by 1957 the company's products included a series of good quality Grand Prix racing cars, Scammell Scarab articulated trucks, farm equipment, and some

military vehicles. DCMT, for its part, decided to sell and market its own toy products and moved into the big league of toymakers under a new trademark: Lone Star.

Lone Star

In an era when schoolchildren spent their spare time charging round the playground pretending to be cowboys and Indians, and TV programmes like *Laramie, Cheyenne* and *The Virginian* had a big following, DCMT's range of 'Wild West' toy guns, holsters and sheriffs' badges quickly struck a chord – helped by a clever marketing campaign that involved a travelling salesman dressed as a cowboy called Steve Larrabee who went round toy shops showing the company's inventory.

Lone Star was always looking for ways of expanding its product line and the company launched a small group of cars under the name 'Road-masters' at the Harrogate Toy Trade Fair in January 1956. The idea was to combine vintage and modern vehicles in gift sets of two, as well as selling them separately. Thus, a 1955 MG TF was paired with a 1912 'Bullnose' Morris – a reminder that the MG marque originated from 'Morris Garages.' Also available were two Daimlers, two Fords, and a 1904 Darracq which had appeared in the film *Genevieve*. The Road-masters were innovative for their time in their use of plastic components but the range did not catch on and was quickly dropped.

Around 1962 Lone Star launched a second generation of Roadmaster cars (now spelt without the hyphen) which were much better finished. These were marketed in the USA by the Tootsietoy company. Most were based on American cars (Chevrolet Corvair, Rambler, Cadillac 62, Ford Sunliner, Chevrolet El Camino Pickup, Dodge Dart) with the addition of a Rolls-Royce Silver Cloud and, rarest of all, a Citroën DS 19.

In 1965 came the smaller Impy series, slightly larger than the Matchbox series, and fitted with many operating features. As much as 80 per cent of production was destined for export. Unfortunately, Impy had barely established itself before the market was shaken up by the arrival of Mattel's Hot Wheels. Matchbox quickly redesigned its own models to compete,

Crescent's most successful entry into the diecast market consisted of a series of racing cars, including the Le Mans-winning Jaguar D Type.

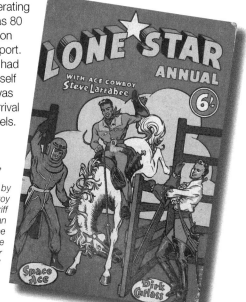

Lone Star prospered by making items like toy guns, holsters and sheriff badges, and issued an annual recounting the adventures of 'Steve Larrabee, the Lone Star rider.'

Roadmaster Impy Super Cars

ONLY 88¢

19 Volvo 1800 S

20 VW Ambulance

21 Fiat 2300 S

23 Alfa Romeo Giulia 1600 Spider

24 Open Truck

27 Ford Taunus 12 M

18 Ford Corsair

The Right-Size Car with ALL these Real-Car Features

16 Police Patrol Car

32 Fire Chief

Lone Star Impy cars were a little larger than Matchbox cars, but smaller than Dinky or Corgi items. Many were exported to the USA where they were advertised in toy store catalogues.

fitting low-friction axles and calling them 'Superfast,' while Lone Star's Impy cars similarly re-emerged as Flyers.

Lone Star made numerous other diecast ranges, such as the Tuf Tots series of small cars and trucks sold as pocket money toys, and the simple, robust Roadmaster Major series of trucks and tractors. Production of various Lone Star diecasts continued into the seventies, notably the Farmer's Boy range of tractors and farm equipment and a simplified and slimmed down Impy range.

Chad Valley

Chad Valley was one of the oldest names in the British toy industry,

having made board games and wooden toys since as far back as 1897. The name comes from the location of the factory in Chad Valley, Harborne near Birmingham. The company produced some clockwork-powered diecast models, mostly Hillmans, Humbers, Sunbeams and Commers which were sold as promotional models in Rootes Group dealerships between 1951 and 1954.

Britains

Britains is, of course, famous as a manufacturer of toy soldiers, but the company also made motor lorries, some sports cars, military vehicles and land speed record cars before the war. With the rise in popularity of OO gauge model railways, Britains introduced the 'Lilliput' series of model vehicles. A 1960 trade catalogue pictures

"Lilliput"
CIVILIAN VEHICLES

METAL
"OO" & "HO" SCALE
TRADE *Britain* MARK
Regd No 459993

LV608   3-ton Farm Lorry. Spare wheel fitted. An extremely well-finished model. In attractive assorted colours
Measures 3¼" long

LV603   Articulated Lorry
Measures 4" long

LV614   Articulated Truck, with spare wheel
Measures 4⅜" long

LV618   Army Ambulance
Measures 3" long

LV617   Local Authority Ambulance
(Cream)
Measures 3" long

LV616   1½-ton Farm or Civilian Truck, with spare wheel
Measures 2¹³⁄₁₆" long

LV619   Post Office Royal Mail Van
Measures 3" long

38

LV603	17/3 doz.	2/6	each ¼ doz.	LV614	21/10 doz.	3/2	each ¼ doz.	LV618	21/10 doz.	3/2	each ¼ doz.
LV608	17/3 doz.	2/6	each ¼ doz.	LV616	17/3 doz.	2/6	each ¼ doz.	LV619	21/10 doz.	3/2	each ¼ doz.
				LV617	21/10 doz.	3/2	each ¼ doz.				

The name of Britains is primarily associated with toy soldiers, but some vehicles were made, too, such as the 'Lilliput' series of OO and HO scale commercial vehicles from 1960.

an open sports car and a closed saloon, a number of commercial vehicles, most of them based on a Fordson chassis, and some military vehicles. In the 1960s Britains also made some Land Rover models to go with its plastic farm toys.

Morestone and Budgie

Morris and Stone (London) Ltd. was one of many North London toy companies to emerge after the Second World War, but it made more of an impact on the diecast market and its products lasted, in

one form or another, into the 1980s. Landmarks in the history of the company include the launch of the 'Esso' series in 1956 (a range of small diecasts inspired by Matchbox and packed in boxes resembling Esso petrol pumps), the introduction of toys based on characters in Enid Blyton's *Noddy* stories and, above all, the launch of Budgie Toys, a series of diecast commercial vehicles, in 1959. The complex story of Morestone and Budgie, and the various changes of ownership involved, has been traced in depth in a book by Robert Newson.

GREAT BRITAIN

Dinky Toys 111 Triumph TR2
The Triumph was available in two versions: 'competition finish' (1956-59) with racing numbers, and driver in overalls and 'touring finish' (1957-62) with civilian driver.
Price guide: £140-£180
(Courtesy David G Ralston)

Dinky Toys 142 Jaguar Mk X
UK issue produced between 1962 and 1968. The opening boot contains plastic luggage. The Jaguar was one of a number of British Dinky models assembled in South Africa by Arthur E Harris (Pty) Ltd and painted in different colours. These variations are extremely rare and can fetch four figure sums at auction.
Price guide (standard UK issue): £75

Dinky Toys American cars
Three of the numerous American cars modelled by Dinky. These must have seemed very exotic to British children in the 1950s. Left-to-right: 170 Ford Fordor (produced 1949 – 59); 172 Studebaker Land Cruiser (1954-59); 171 Hudson Commodore (1950-59).
Price guide: Ford: £150-£300;Studebaker: £180-£260; Hudson £100-£200

Dinky Toys 176 Austin A105
It took two years for Dinky to catch up with Corgi and fit window glazing to its cars, the first being this Austin A105 which was produced from 1958 until 1963. Later versions with spun wheel hubs are the hardest to find.
Price guide: £90-£250

Dinky Toys 165 Humber Hawk
In addition to windows the Humber boasted another innovation: suspension. The car was made from 1959 until 1963 and can also be found in cream/maroon.
Price guide: £90-£140

Dinky Toys 181 Volkswagen
The Dinky Volkswagen had a lengthy production run (from 1956 until 1969), no doubt because it sold well in different export markets. The final issues had spun wheels and came in a red/yellow box without a picture of the car.
Price guide: £80-£120

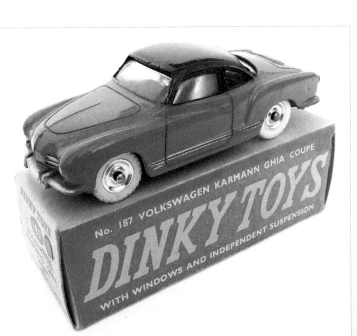

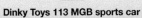

Dinky Toys 187 Volkswagen Karmann Ghia
The stylish Karmann Ghia coupé was based on the Volkswagen Beetle. The Dinky model, produced between 1959 and 1964, comes in red/black or green/cream, and can also be found in the French Dinky range.
Price guide: £80

Dinky Toys 113 MGB sports car
Close co-operation between Meccano Limited and the British Motor Corporation enabled this MGB model to be launched on the same day as the real car in September 1962. It also boasted a 'first' for Dinky: opening side doors.
Price guide: £70

GREAT BRITAIN

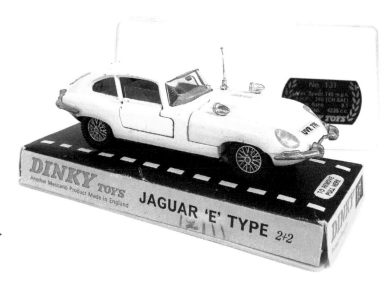

Dinky Toys 184 Volvo 122S
Although it is usually found in red, there are also extremely rare variations of the Volvo in both white and cream.
Price guide: £90 (red); £180 (white)

Dinky Toys 131 Jaguar E Type 2+2
This model is typical of late 1960s Dinkies as the doors, bonnet and boot open. It was first issued in cream (1968-70). Thereafter, several metallic colours were used until production ceased in 1977.
Price guide: £60-£90

Dinky Toys 273 RAC Mini van
The Mini van was available in the colours of the two British roadside assistance organisations, the AA and the RAC. Both versions had opening rear doors and a roof sign made of plastic. Produced 1965-70.
Price guide: £190

Dinky Toys 129 Volkswagen 1300
Produced for eleven years from 1965 onwards, the VW originally had spun wheels, later changed to the 'Speedwheels' type in 1972. Again, all parts open.
Price guide: £35-£50

Dinky Toys 482 Bedford van 'Kodak'
Three liveries were available on the Bedford van: 'Kodak' (1954-56), 'Dinky Toys' (1956-60) and 'Ovaltine' (1955-60).
Price guide: £150

Dinky Toys 255 Mersey Tunnel Land Rover
The cover of the 1956 Dinky catalogue depicted the entrance to Liverpool's Mersey Tunnel, where this Land Rover was deployed as a patrol vehicle. The model was produced 1955-61.
Price guide: £60

Dinky Toys 514 Guy van 'Spratt's'
Six different liveries were available on the Guy van: Spratts, Lyons, Slumberland, Weetabix, Ever Ready and Golden Shred. The van was available in Spratt's colours between 1953 and 1956.
Price guide: £250+

Dinky Toys 522 Big Bedford lorry
In production from 1952 until 1963, the Bedford lorry is usually found in maroon/beige colours; this rare blue/yellow combination dates from between 1952 and 1954.
Price guide: £150
(Courtesy David G Ralston)

GREAT BRITAIN

Dinky Supertoys 923 Big Bedford van 'Heinz'
Larger commercial vehicles were classified as 'Dinky Supertoys.' From 1955 until 1958 this model carried a picture of Heinz beans, replaced with a sauce bottle in 1958-59.
Price guide: £250 (first version): £1000+ (later version).
(Courtesy David G Ralston)

Dinky Toys 987 ABC TV control room and 281 *Pathé News* camera car
These camera vehicles demonstrate Dinky's willingness to recycle existing models. The ABC TV Control room (left), issued in 1962, had already appeared in dark green BBC livery in 1959. The Pathé News car, dating from 1967, is a reworking of the Fiat Station Wagon (no. 172) from 1965. The camera operator is the same on both models, though the camera is different.
Price guide: ABC: £200; Pathé News: £110

Dinky Supertoys 966 Marrel multi-bucket unit and 960 cement mixer
Two models on the building and construction theme. The multi-bucket transporter (produced between 1960 and 1964) is based on a Leyland cab unit, whereas the cement mixer (1960-68) is an Albion.
Price guide: 960: £80; 966: £100

Mettoy Castoys Royal Mail van
This heavy diecast Morris van first appeared as part of Mettoy's 'Castoys' series in 1948 but made a comeback in 1957 as a Royal Mail van. Other liveries include BOAC (blue) and Post Office Telephones (green). Length: 6 inches.
Price guide: £300
(Courtesy Bruce Sterling)

Corgi Toys 205 Riley Pathfinder
The Riley, released in 1956, was one of the first batch of Corgi cars fitted with window glazing. It came in either red or dark blue, and could be purchased with or without a friction motor.
Price guide: £95

Corgi Toys 352 RAF Standard Vanguard
The civilian Standard Vanguard was added to the Corgi range in 1957, to be followed by an RAF version in 1958.
Price guide: £95

Corgi Toys 214 Ford Thunderbird
Like Dinky, Corgi modelled cars which would appeal to the North American market. The first was a Studebaker Golden Hawk, followed by this Ford Thunderbird in 1959. Later in the same year, a convertible version was added.
Price guide: £90

Corgi Toys 230 Mercedes-Benz 220SE Coupé
Corgi models increasingly featured opening parts, such as the boot on this Mercedes. The model was introduced in 1962 and renumbered 253 in 1964. It has been seen in cream, metallic red, dark blue and black.
Price guide: £75+

GREAT BRITAIN

Corgi Toys 349 Morris Mini Minor 'Pop Art'
The decorations on this Mini reflected the hippy culture of the 1960s. According to Marcel van Cleemput, Corgi's Chief Designer, only a few examples were produced and the model was never officially listed in any catalogue.
Price guide: £1000-£1500
(Courtesy Gary Cohen)

Corgi Toys 'The Beatles' Car
To cash in on the popularity of The Beatles, an existing Corgi model of a Superior Ambulance on a Cadillac chassis was modified and fitted with four plastic figures, but the proposal was rejected by Corgi's management. This sample belonged to Marcel van Cleemput and was sold at auction by Sotheby's. It is impossible to give a value for such a unique piece.
(Courtesy Gary Cohen)

Corgi Toys 475 Citroën Safari
This 1964 Olympic Winter Sports model came with a roof rack, skis and figure. Other versions of the Citroën include 'Corgi Ski Club' and '1968 Grenoble Winter Olympics.'
Price guide: Olympics: £100; Ski Club: £125

Corgi Toys 252 Rover 2000 and 259 Citroën Le Dandy
The stylish 2000, a very modern design compared to previous Rovers, was a natural subject for Corgi to choose. By contrast, the Citroën Le Dandy, a coupé built on the DS chassis by French coachbuilder Henri Chapron, would have been a rare sight on British roads. Corgi introduced the Rover in 1963 and the Citroën in 1966.
Price guide: Rover: £75; Citroën: £115

Corgi Toys 441 Volkswagen 'Toblerone' van
*A reworking of the previous year's plain VW van, this 1963 version featured
'Trans-o-lite' headlamps. Light entering the panel on the roof was transmitted,
via clear plastic rods, to the headlamps which then appeared to light up.*
Price guide: £100+

Corgi Toys 261 Aston Martin DB5 *James Bond*
*The most famous ever Corgi model, and the one which every schoolboy of the 1960s
remembers, the Aston Martin from the film Goldfinger set new sales records, exceeding
five million units. With its ingenious mechanisms – ejector seat, front machine guns and
rear bullet-proof shield – the Aston secured Corgi's dominance of the diecast market
and was to lead to many similar 'character merchandise' toys in the years to come.*
Price guide: £195+

Corgi Toys 336 Toyota *James Bond*
*Corgi continued to exploit the James Bond theme in 1967 with the Toyota 2000GT from
You Only Live Twice. A button made the bootlid spring open, and pressing down the car
released four missiles.*
Price guide: £250

Corgi Toys Gift Set 41
*A Scammel Transporter with six cars, including three minis and a rare MGC in
orange. This very rare set was available by mail order.*
Price guide: £700+
(Courtesy Gary Cohen)

Matchbox 56 London trolleybus
In production between 1958 and 1965, the trolleybus carried advertising decals reading 'Drink Peardrax.'
Price guide: £40+

Matchbox 57 Wolseley 1500
Produced from 1958 until 1961, the Wolseley was a car that other toy manufacturers of the period overlooked.
Price guide: £40

Matchbox Series
(Left-to-right): 34 Volkswagen delivery van (1957-62); 46 Pickford's removals van (1960-68); 70 Ford Thames estate car (1959-66).
Price guide: VW: £25-£45; Pickford's: £80; Ford: £30.

Matchbox 33 Ford Zodiac and A1 BP petrol pump set
The BP petrol pumps, dating from 1963, are one of several accessory packs offered to accompany Matchbox vehicles. The Zodiac originally appeared in 1957 in a dark green colour, with this two-tone version replacing it in 1959.
Price guide: Zodiac: £120; petrol pumps: £20

Matchbox M7 Ford Thames Trader cattle truck
The Matchbox Major Pack series comprised larger, usually articulated, commercial vehicles, such as this cattle truck from 1960.
Price guide: £50

Spot-On 100/100SL Ford Zodiac
The first saloon car in the 1959 Spot-On range was the Ford Zodiac, and it was issued in many different single and two-tone colour schemes. No. 100SL is another version with front and rear lights powered by a battery inserted in a compartment underneath the car.
Price guide: £150+

Spot-On 112 Jensen 541
One strength of the Spot-On range was the inclusion of original and less common vehicles, such as this Jensen coupé, which, in real life, had bodywork made from glass fibre.
Price guide: £150+

Spot-On 102 Bentley Continental Sports Saloon
An elegant four-door sports saloon which, like all other Spot-On models, is to 1/42 scale, making it look very large indeed when placed next to Dinky or Corgi cars.
Price guide: £180+

GREAT BRITAIN

Spot-On Mercedes-Benz 230SL
This unusual combination of Mercedes with horse trailer is believed to have been part of a batch of models made up using surplus boxes and accessories and exported to the USA.
Price guide: £400+
(Courtesy Gary Cohen)

Spot-On 260 Royal Rolls-Royce
This magnificent Royal Rolls-Royce features electric lights and an opening boot, and comes with figures of Queen Elizabeth II and Prince Philip in the rear. There are many small detail components, hence the high price of examples in mint condition.
Price guide: £300+

Spot-On 111a/1 Ford Thames Trader articulated flat float
This model, dating from 1959, is in the maroon and cream livery of British Railways and carries a sack load. The car in the foreground is the Austin-Healey, shown in a rare two-tone colour scheme.
Price guide: £300+ each
(Courtesy Bruce Sterling)

Spot-On 120 Fiat Multipla
Based on the Fiat 600 saloon, the six-seater Multipla was often used as a taxi in Italy. Like most Spot-On models, it came in a wide range of colours.
Price guide: £140+
(Courtesy Bruce Sterling)

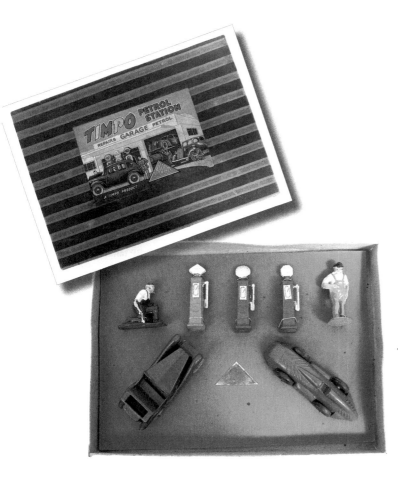

Spot-On Trucks

In addition to the Thames Trader (left), Spot-On made numerous trucks with (left-to-right) ERF, AEC Mammoth and Austin cabs.
Price guide: £250 each
(Courtesy Bruce Sterling)

Timpo Petrol Station set

A rare 1940s gift set containing an MG T series and a racing car, accompanied by three petrol pumps and two mechanics.
Price guide: £150

Charbens Scammell lorry

Half a century ago the 'mechanical horse' was a common sight in railway goods yards. This brown and cream example is in the livery of the GWR (Great Western Railway) and, as such, pre-dates the nationalisation of British Railways in 1948. Like many cheaper diecast toys, it did not come individually boxed but in trade packs of six.
Price guide: £35

Charbens cable drum lorry

Charbens had a long history of making metal soldiers and farm animals, but the company also made numerous vehicles in the early postwar period. This cable drum lorry had a winding handle to lower the rear platform. Unfortunately, most surviving examples suffer from metal fatigue.
Price guide: £50

GREAT BRITAIN

Crescent 1276 Scammell Scarab Shell-BP tanker
The best known Crescent diecasts were a series of Grand Prix racing cars dating from the 1956-58 period, but a few commercial vehicles were also made, such as this Scammell Scarab tanker.
Price guide: £100

Crescent 'Dial 999' set
This early postwar set contains a saloon car, loosely based on a Jaguar, and figures of policemen, one of whom has a dog, pursuing robbers. It evokes the atmosphere of 1940s crime films like The Blue Lamp and the TV police series Dixon of Dock Green, both of which starred Jack Warner. It is rare to find a complete boxed set.
Price guide: £150

Crescent Dexta tractor and trailer
Based on a Fordson prototype, the 5-inch long Dexta tractor was added to the range in 1967.
Price guide: £90

River Series Buick
Loosely based on a 1953 Buick, this rather crudely made toy can be found with or without a friction motor. It is very rare to find one with its original box.
Price guide: £100

River Series Esso tanker
The River Series contained numerous trucks with the same chassis and different rear sections.
Price guide: £60

Shackleton Foden lorries
Shackleton was a small family firm based in Sandbach, Cheshire, which made some diecast Foden lorries between 1958 and 1962. These were around 12 inches in length and could be dismantled and re-assembled. They are extremely rare today.
Price guide: £300
(Courtesy Bruce Sterling)

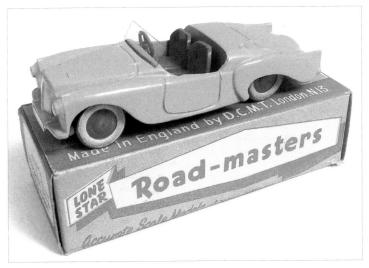

Lone Star Road-masters Daimler Conquest
Part of the short-lived Road-masters series of 1956, this Daimler is highly desirable as it wasn't modelled by any other diecast manufacturer of the period.
Price guide: £100

Lone Star Road-masters MG TF
Introduced in 1956 and on sale for only a short time, this model is much sought-after by MG enthusiasts. It has been seen in red, yellow, metallic light green and metallic light or dark blue, with or without racing numbers.
Price guide: £100

GREAT BRITAIN

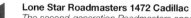

Lone Star Roadmasters 1472 Cadillac
The second-generation Roadmasters appeared in 1960 and originally came in picture boxes, like this Cadillac. The models were sold in the USA under the Tootsietoys name.
Price guide: £70

Lone Star Roadmasters 1474 Chevrolet El Camino
The El Camino pick-up also appeared in the Dinky Toys range, but the Lone Star had the added refinement of an opening rear tailgate.
Price guide: £60

Lone Star 1479 Chevrolet Corvair 'Feuerwehr'
Later issues of the Roadmasters had white plastic tyres and came in yellow 'window' boxes. The Corvair is relatively common, but this 'Feuerwehr' version is harder to find as it was made for export to Germany.
Price guide: £80

Lone Star Roadmasters 1482 Citroën DS19
The Citroën was the last to be added to the Roadmasters series and is today the most sought-after.
Price guide: £80

Lone Star Impy
The Impy range dates from 1966 and consists of 3-inch long cars which, in terms of scale, fitted somewhere between Matchbox and Dinky size. Pictured here are: 15 Volkswagen Microbus and 28 Peugeot 404 (back row); 10 Jaguar Mark X and 27 Ford Taunus 12M (front row).
Price guide: £25-£30 each

Lone Star Roadmaster Major Austin articulated trucks
The Roadmaster Majors were a series of simple, robust commercial vehicles, many based on an Austin cab unit. They came shrink-wrapped rather than individually boxed.
Price guide: £20

Morestone double decker bus
Clearly based on the well-known Dinky Toys model, this bus was issued between 1955 and 1958. Three variations of the 'Esso' transfer have been identified.
Price guide: £75

Morestone Foden express delivery wagon
One of four variants on the 8-wheel Foden chassis, issued in 1955. The others are a flat truck with chains, an open lorry, and an 'Esso' tanker.
Price guide: £100

GREAT BRITAIN

Morestone *Noddy* gift set
Enid Blyton's series of children's stories featuring Noddy and Big Ears was extremely popular in the 1950s, and this rare and desirable Morestone set is an early example of 'character merchandising.' The bicycle and car are of diecast metal while the figures are plastic. The car is 2 inches long.
Price guide: £200+

Morestone 'Esso' Series
In 1956 Morestone made an arrangement with the Esso Petrol Company to issue a range of small Matchbox-size cars in boxes that resemble Esso petrol pumps. Pictured here are (left-to-right): Austin-Healey, Wolseley police car and Volkswagen.
Price guide: £25 each

Budgie Toys 258 Daimler ambulance
The Daimler was the classic 1950s ambulance. This Budgie version has opening doors and first appeared in 1956. The original tooling survived and the model can still be found in kit form today.
Price guide: £40–£50

Budgie Toys 290 Bedford Tonibell ice cream van
A difficult item to find because of its short production run – between 1963 and 1964. The cow on the roof is often missing.
Price guide: £150

Budgie Toys 236 Routemaster Bus and 296 Midland Red Coach
Midland Red coaches provided a motorway service between Birmingham and London. The Budgie model dates from 1963 and was also issued in a blue and cream 'Blue Line Sightseeing Co' livery for export to the USA. The Routemaster dates from 1960 and had a long production run, being sold in London souvenir shops for many years.
Price guide: Routemaster: £20; Midland Red coach: £50; Sightseeing coach: £125+

Benbros Mighty Midgets
The influence of the Matchbox series is obvious in these 'Mighty Midgets.' Left-to-right: AA Land Rover, Bedford milk float and Daimler ambulance.
Price guide: £25-£40 each

Benbros farm tractor and log cart
The Benbros tractor was supplied with various attachments, and can also be found with a covered cab and a shovel at the front. The tractor is believed to represent a Ferguson prototype. The artwork on the box is particularly colourful.
Price guide: £75

TP modern flat lorry
TP stands for Toy Products, which was located in Walsall. Around 1946 the company made a number of simple diecast cars and lorries, including this 5-inch flat lorry. Price guide: £50
(Courtesy Douglas R Kelly)

Chad Valley Humber Hawk
This model is one of a number of promotional items sold in Rootes Group showrooms in the early 1950s. It is powered by a clockwork motor.
Price guide: £150

Brimtoy Bedford artic flat truck
Brimtoy made many Bedford trucks which combined a tinplate body with a plastic cab unit, but this example is unusual as the cab is diecast metal. A key can be inserted underneath to wind up the clockwork motor.
Price guide: £90

Chad Valley Lyon's Ice Cream van
Three different liveries are known to have appeared on this Guy van: 'Chad Valley,' 'Guy Motors Ltd' and 'Lyons Ice Cream.' The rear doors are made of tinplate and can be opened.
Price guide: £200

Wardie petrol pump set
A rare boxed set of petrol pumps from B and J Ward of London, which distributed numerous accessory items designed to accompany toy cars and model railway layouts.
Price guide: £100

FRANCE

When Meccano Limited opened a factory at Bobigny in the outskirts of Paris, the Dinky Toy range caught on as quickly in France as it had across the English channel. However, several other companies were already producing toy cars in France, and French Dinky never enjoyed a monopoly of the market like its British counterpart.

Although much of the early history of French diecast remains obscure, it is known that companies identified by initials such as 'AR,' 'CD' and 'SR' made simple diecast toy vehicles in the 1920s. Initially, some of these looked similar to American Tootsietoys, but models of French cars soon began to appear, such as AR's Peugeot 201, 301 and 601, and Renault 40CV delivery van.

Solido

In 1929 Ferdinand de Vazeilles, owner of a pressure diecasting business in Nanterre, suggested to one of his clients in the car components industry that he could make a small wheeled toy which might be used to promote Gergovia sparkplugs ('bougie' in French). That strange little item led to the Solido series of metal diecast cars. Described as 'Automobiles à Transformation,' they could be taken apart and different bodies fitted to the same chassis powered by a clockwork motor. The earliest body styles comprised a streamlined 'Torpedo' racing car, a coupé, closed cabriolet, saloon, lorry, van, single deck coach, and something described as an 'Autobus Anglais à Imperiale' – a kind of double deck bus with open seats on the roof. These were not exact replicas of real vehicles, but they did resemble the style of the cars of the prewar period.

This early group of Solidos was known as the 140 series because the chassis was 140 millimetres in length. Soon afterwards, a smaller 100mm 'Junior' series appeared.

After Solido moved to a new factory at Ivry-la-Bataille in 1938, new cars were added to the Junior range which continued to be developed further after the war. The cars were now based on recognisable prototypes though they were not named as such, being identified instead by the names of French towns. Thus, the Cadillac carries the name Vichy, the Delahaye is called after Antibes, and the Packard is named Royan.

Dinky Toys

Although Solido was already established by the time Dinky reached the French market in 1934, the two ranges were not in direct competition as the Dinkies were smaller and cheaper and did not have clockwork motors. Some Dinky Toys were imported from Liverpool while others were made in the French Meccano factory. The French Dinky expert Jean-Michel Roulet has pointed out that Meccano France was at this time "quite firmly ruled from Binns Road" and, as a result, most French Dinkies were similar to English ones, even when made from separate moulds at the Bobigny site. Nevertheless, some models of French vehicles were made before the war, the first being a Peugeot 402, also available as a taxi. Other distinctive French subjects included the small Simca 5, and a model of the famous green and white Paris bus.

After the war French Dinky further developed its own identity. From 1949 onwards new models of postwar French cars started to appear, such as the Ford Vedette, Citroën Traction Avant, Peugeot

Typical period artwork on the cover of the 1955 French Dinky Toys catalogue.

DINKY TOYS
ET
DINKY SUPERTOYS
Marques déposées

ESSO

Jean MASSÉ

Fabriqués en France par MECCANO - Paris

Jean Massé's design for the 1959 edition of the Dinky catalogue incorporates some artistic touches.

203, Citroën 2CV and Simca Aronde. Unlike British Dinky, however, the French range did not have the market to itself.

CIJ

In 1950 another diecast series was launched: CIJ. The letters stand for the 'Compagnie Industrielle du Jouet' whose history stretched back to 1878 when Albert Migault started a small toy business in Paris. In 1919 he was joined by Marcel Gourdet, a tinsmith from the town of Briare, in the Loiret region. An example of Gourdet's ingenuity was a toy fish that he devised in 1920, able to swim fifty metres thanks to a clockwork motor that was operated by winding a handle inside its mouth! Two years later, Gourdet made some 1/10th scale replicas of

Citroën cars, and when Albert Migault's son Fernand showed these to the motor magnate André Citroën he was so impressed that he immediately placed a large order.

On the strength of this order Migault and Gourdet built a new factory at Briare in 1923 and the company expanded rapidly, assuming the name CIJ in 1930. But disaster followed in 1931 as the contract came to an abrupt end when the Citroën car company plunged into financial crisis. CIJ was soon back on track in 1934 when it negotiated another deal with the rival Renault company, which was only too glad to profit from Citroën's difficulties. CIJ now concentrated on making tinplate 'Jouets Renault.'

For the next thirty years CIJ had exclusive rights to manufacture

les plus finies des miniatures

voici
les
dernières
nouveautés

EUROPARC

créées par la
Compagnie
Industrielle
du Jouet

I D BREAK CITROEN
Avec suspension, glaces
et aménagements
intérieurs.

FACELLIA
Petite place réel utilisé par
la capote. Suspension et aménagements intérieurs.

déjà l'AMI 6 CITROEN
Remarquable de fidélité !
Avec glaces,
banquettes et suspension.

MICROCAR ESTAFETTE
Toutes
les portières
s'ouvrent.
Banquettes,
tableau de bord
et glaces.

ESTAFETTE POLICE
La première miniature
électrifiée.
Le phare du toit
clignote
lorsque
la voiture roule !

CHARIOT "ZONE BLEUE"
Comme le modèle réel utilisé par
la police parisienne, ce chariot
permet l'enlèvement d'une voiture
en stationnement interdit.

CIJ

**Compagnie
Industrielle du
Jouet**

An early 1960s advertisement for the CIJ Europarc series.

models of Renault vehicles – a distinct advantage when, in 1950, it launched a new diecast series with the Renault 4CV as the inaugural model. This was the perfect choice of car for the period, as it was the little rear-engined 4CV that brought motoring to the masses in postwar France. Little wonder that some 400,000 examples of the toy were made. It was followed by a model of the flagship of Renault's range, the Frégate, and many other Renault cars, vans and trucks, in addition to a number of other French cars by Peugeot and Panhard, and the occasional German and American car, too.

CIJ declined in popularity after 1957, the year when Marcel Gourdet finally left the firm at the age of 84. A change of ownership in 1960 led to an attempted relaunch under the name 'CIJ Europarc,' but production does not seem to have lasted beyond 1967.

JRD

Confusingly, JRD is another company whose history is closely linked to CIJ. The letters are the initials of Monsieur Jean Rabier Donot who was in charge of Jouets Citroën until 1934. He set up his own company in

1938 but retained his connections with the Citroën marque. After the war JRD brought out a tinplate model of the Citroën 2CV and, around 1956, launched a diecast range. JRD continued to offer tinplate and diecast models of Citroën cars and vans throughout the 1950s. JRD disappeared in the mid-1960s, and remaining stock was taken over by the already struggling CIJ brand which issued surplus models in CIJ boxes.

Another twist to this complex story occurred when, twenty years later, the original JRD moulds for the Citroën Traction Avant, DS, H van and 2CV resurfaced and were put back into operation. Fortunately, these are inscribed with the year of production, '85,' to avoid confusion with original issues.

Quiralu

As if the French toy car market was not overcrowded enough, yet another attempt was made to launch a 1/43 scale diecast series. In the 1930s a Monsieur Quirin, a manufacturer of aluminium saucepans in Luxeuil, Haute Saône, diversified into toy manufacture with a series of metal solders and farm figures under the name Quiralu (a combination of 'Quirin' and 'aluminium'). Quiralu started making diecast vehicles in 1956 and although the series included just twelve basic car and van castings and a couple of larger trucks, some unusual and original subjects were chosen. The Peugeot 403 and Simca Vedette are rather uninspiring, but the Rolls-Royce Silver Cloud with Hooper bodywork, the Jaguar XK 140 convertible, and the two bubble cars (Messerschmitt and Isetta Velam) are very desirable. Production seems to have lasted just a few years but – as happened with the JRD Citroëns – the original Quiralu tooling survived and the range has been reissued by another French company, Louis Surber SA, maker of the Eligor range.

Solido 100 Series

One factor that contributed to the decline of CIJ, JRD and Quiralu was the launch of the Solido 100 Series in 1957. Unlike previous Solido products, this range comprised more realistic non-motorised cars in 1/43 scale. The effect in France can be likened to the impact made in the UK by the arrival of Corgi. Corgi's idea was to fit window glazing; Solido, for its part, came up with spring suspension. The initial theme of the Solido 100 series (so-called because of the catalogue numbering sequence used) was sports and racing cars, the first being the Jaguar D Type. The choice of a British rather than a French car may seem strange but the success of the Jaguar at Le Mans would have made it very familiar in France. Sales figures proved it to be an inspired choice: the model remained in production for fourteen years and, according to French Solido historian Bertrand Azéma, over one million were produced. Early Solido issues also included a number of convertibles: the Simca Oceane, Mercedes 190SL, Peugeot 403, Renault Floride and Alfa Romeo Giulietta, all of which came with either a male or female driver moulded in plastic.

In 1961 the range expanded to take in GT (Grand Tourisme) coupés such as the Ferrari 250GT and Lancia Flaminia, and opening parts began to be fitted. Next, Solido launched the 'Age d'Or' series of vintage cars in 1963. The idea was, of course, similar to the 1956

solido

◄ **CABRIOLET PEUGEOT 403**
1468 cm³ - Vitesse 140 km/h.

COOPER 1500 cm³ ►
1ʳᵉ au
Grand Prix de Monaco 1958

◄ **CABRIOLET SIMCA "OCÉANE"**
1290 cm³ - Vitesse 140 km/h.

miniatures *solido* sont munies de la fameuse suspension — Toutes les miniatures ...

Solido's 100 series specialised in models of sports and racing cars.

launched the metal-bodied 'Jet-Car' series in 1971, while continuing to offer many of the same models in plastic.

France Jouets

This company, often referred to by its initials FJ, originated in Marseilles in 1946. FJ made numerous large scale plastic vehicles powered by electric or friction motors, branching into diecast in the early 1960s with a series of military and civilian trucks in around 1/60 scale. Although about 100 models were produced, almost all of them are variations on a mere half dozen basic castings – Dodge, GMC, Berliet GAK, Berliet Stradair, Jeep and, most impressive of all, a Pacific low loader which, at fourteen inches in length, was more than three times the size of most other FJ models.

After FJ went out of business in 1975 the tooling for some models was reused by another French firm, Safir, which had originally made a series of veteran cars. Under the new name of Champion the Berliet

A selection of Berliet Trucks from the 1960 FJ (France Jouets) catalogue.

Matchbox Yesteryear series, and a range of veteran and vintage vehicles had already been launched in France in 1958 by RAMI (Les Rétrospectives Automobiles Miniatures). However, the Solidos were superior in detail and finish, were made to a consistent 1/43 scale, and tended to be based on prestigious vehicles, like the 1930 Bugatti Royale, the 1926 Hispano Suiza, or the 1934 Voisin 17CV.

Solido's success in France was to hasten the demise of the French Dinky range in 1971, whereas in Britain Dinky struggled on until the end of the decade. Since then, Solido has not been without its troubles, but the brand has survived to this day, though production now takes place in China.

Norev

In 1953 Monsieur Joseph Veron started producing 1/43 scale plastic cars in Lyon, reversing the letters of his surname to create 'Norev.' The Norev range was successful as it offered Dinky-size cars at lower prices than metal ones. However, by the late sixties sales were declining: children were becoming more demanding and plastic cars seemed like cheap substitutes compared to the increasingly sophisticated diecasts. Norev then

BERLIET G.A.K.

Réf. 111 Gak Fourragère

Réf. 109 Gak Semat

Réf. 104 Gak Carrier

Réf. 114 Gak Livraison Domicile

Réf. 116 Gak Multibenne

Réf. 107 Gak Bétonneuse

Réf. 108 Gak Grue

Réf. 110 Gak E.D.F.

trucks, Jeeps and military vehicles re-emerged in 1975 in a modified form using more plastic parts and brighter decals.

Small-scale

The Matchbox concept produced many imitators in France, just as it did in the UK. In about 1956 a road roller, excavator, dumper truck and Caterpillar tractor went on sale under the name of Jadali, all copied directly from Matchbox products. The following year, the Gitanes brand was launched, and sold in boxes that even looked liked matchboxes. Of the eight models in this series, two were Matchbox copies, a Massey Harris tractor, and a caravan. The others were typically French and are more desirable today, especially the Citroën DS 19, Citroën 2CV, Simca Versailles, Renault Dauphine and 1000kg van.

Next came Midget Toys in 1959. Apart from a few uninspiring trucks, this series contained another Citroën DS, a Panhard Dyna in saloon and convertible form, a Vanwall and Jaguar D Type racer and another Massey Harris Tractor. The most original product was a Vespa 400, a small city car designed by Piaggio, famous for its Vespa scooters. Midget Toys made this in both 1/43 and 1/86 scales. Another miniature range was made up of fifteen commercial vehicles and called Les Routiers. In addition to some Simca, Panhard and Citroën trucks, the range included vehicles like a road grader, an excavator and a Richier road roller. The most sought-after issues are two unusual publicity vehicles associated with the Tour de France bicycle race. One is shaped liked a barrel advertising the aperitif Byrrh and the other represents a tube of Vitabrill hair cream.

In addition to these minor manufacturers, CIJ offered a series of ten Micro-Miniatures packed in transparent plastic cylinders rather than boxes. Produced for a mere two years (1957-59), these clearly made little impact. It was not until the launch of Majorette in 1965 that small-scale diecasts really caught on in France – to such an extent that they overtook the more established 1/43 scale brands.

Majorette

The story of Majorette is a complicated one involving a bewildering number of changes of ownership, and overlaps with many other famous names in the toy industry. It all began with a difference of opinion between two brothers, Joseph and Emile Veron. Emile worked alongside his older brother in the Norev company, handling the export side of the business. But by 1960 the two disagreed over the future direction the firm was to take. The upshot was that Emile left to start his own company, Rail Route, with the idea of making non-motorised toy trains and associated road vehicles. The trains were not a success but the vehicles were. These were sold under the name Majorette from 1965 onwards and were in some ways similar to Matchbox toys of the period – with added French flair!

The earliest issues consisted of Formula One racing cars (BRM, Porsche, Ferrari) and a number of commercial vehicles with a Bernard cab. The first saloon car was a three-inch long Citroën DS, the most distinctive French car of the period, and consequently one of the most sought-after Majorette models. Like most other French manufacturers, Majorette tended to favour indigenous car manufacturers, and plenty of other Citroëns, Peugeots and Renaults followed. However, Majorette was also good at selecting more original subjects, such as the 'Etalmobile,' an elongated mobile shop with an opening side canopy characteristic of the type of van seen at French food markets.

At the height of its success in the 1980s Majorette was making 400,000 cars a day and eventually took over the long-established but ailing Solido company. One result of this was that French diecasts returned to their roots, as, under Emile Veron's ownership, some of the old Solido 100 Series models were reissued as part of a separate collectors' series under a new name, Verem, in 1985.

Who would have thought that a difference of opinion between two brothers that occurred nearly half a century earlier would have changed the course of the French diecast toy industry?

'Les ré-éditions'

An interesting aspect of the French diecast industry seems to be that a remarkable number of classic models have been reissued. In 1985 the original moulds for JRD Citroën cars and vans were put back into operation, and since then many new liveries have appeared on these. In the same year, the Solido company reissued earlier models from the 100 series under the Verem name, in some cases with extra detailing. The original moulds for the Quiralu range also exist, and these were reused by Louis Surber SA, maker of the Eligor range. The Norev company has similarly produced better finished versions of earlier models.

The latest trend has been for near-identical replicas of 1950s diecasts to be made in China from new tooling. Norev has relaunched many CIJ models and is now developing a new line based on Spot-On, while Dan Toys has reproduced some rare French Dinky Toys items. Atlas Publishing also offers a series of reproduction 1950s Dinky Toys models sold by subscription.

In most cases these models can clearly be identified as modern products and the values of rare originals do not seem to have been adversely affected.

A reissue of the 1950s Jaguar XK 140, made from the original Quiralu moulds. The only significant difference is that the base is unpainted, rather than black, as on the originals.

FRANCE

CIJ 3/10 Volkswagen
Introduced in 1954, the Volkswagen is a good replica of the real car, though it is often finished in rather dull colours. The model is hardest to find in red or in the cream shade pictured.
Price guide: £100+

CIJ 3/15 Chrysler Windsor
One of only two American cars in the CIJ range (the other being a Plymouth Belvedere), the Chrysler was introduced in 1956 and can be found in two-tone blue or two-tone green.
Price guide: £80

CIJ 3/5 Panhard Dyna Junior
CIJ brought out this model in 1955, two years after the appearance of the real car which derived from the Dyna saloon. The tinplate hood is removable.
Price guide: £100

CIJ 3/54 Panhard Dyna Z
The Panhard Dyna was claimed to be a six-seater, though it had a modest two-cylinder engine. The CIJ model, introduced in 1955, comes in various shades of blue, green and grey. 3/54T was the same car in red and black taxi livery.
Price guide: £100

CIJ 3/52 Renault Frégate Grand Pavois

Although the CIJ range already included a model of the large Renault saloon, a new casting based on the luxury 'Grand Pavois' model appeared in two-tone colours in 1958.
Price guide: £200

CIJ 3/54 Renault Break de Chasse

The Renault Manoir was an estate car version of the Frégate saloon. The wood trim effect is achieved by a complex three-stage paint masking operation.
Price guide: £120

CIJ 3/60A Renault 1000kg van 'Astra'

The Renault 1000kg came in many different guises, either as a delivery van or as a public service vehicle with side windows. This rare version, in the livery of 'Astra' margarine, was supplied in a special box.
Price guide: £200

CIJ 3/68PB Renault Dauphinoise 'Postes belges'

Again, the smaller Dauphinoise came in numerous guises: Police, Postes, estate car, etc. This red livery was made for the Belgian market and is one of the rarest CIJ models.
Price guide: £350

FRANCE

CIJ 3/89B Citroën H Van 'Brandt'

After the demise of JRD, CIJ took over some of the models and issued them in CIJ boxes. Production quantities were small, and sometimes existing boxes were simply overlabelled, as in the case of this rare promotional van for Brandt, an electrical goods retailer.
Price guide: £250

CIJ 3/56T Renault Dauphine Taxi

This taxi version of the Dauphine is rarer than the ordinary saloon, partly because of the fragile roof sign and meter. It also comes in two-tone cream and green and was introduced in 1958.
Price guide: £175

CIJ 3/7 Simca 1000

An extremely rare promotional item commemorating the launch of the model on 17 April 1962, the same day as the real car. Only 350 of these were made, packed in boxes with a special label.
Price guide: £400+

CIJ 3/92 Renault Estafette Hostellerie du Cheval Blanc

By 1961 CIJ was producing much more sophisticated models, such as this Renault Estafette minibus which has a sliding side entrance and a rear door that opens in three sections, as on the real vehicle.
Price guide: £100

CIJ 3/94 Renault 2.5 T 'Evian'

One of the most attractive CIJ models is this Renault 2.5 tonne in the livery of 'Evian' mineral water – complete with twelve plastic crates of bottles. It dates from 1962.
Price guide: £250

CIJ 3/65 Chariot de Police Zone Bleue

Introduced in 1964, this pick-up was a late entry in the CIJ range and is modified from an earlier model, the Renault Prairie estate car. The vehicle was designed to tow away illegally parked cars.
Price guide: £200

JRD Peugeot 404

One of the last models to be issued as a JRD, this casting later appeared in red after the CIJ takeover. It is fitted with seats, windows and suspension.
Price guide: £125

JRD Mercedes-Benz 220SE

The Mercedes was modelled by many different firms but the JRD is one of the most successful at capturing the 'presence' of the real car.
Price guide: £125
(Courtesy David G Ralston)

FRANCE

JRD Berliet 'Kronenbourg'
JRD's most impressive commercial vehicles are the various trucks with advertising decals, such as the Unic 'Hafa Oil' van, the Berliet GAK 'Prefontaines' drinks truck, and this articulated Berliet TLR 'Kronenbourg' beer truck.
Price guide: £275
(Courtesy David G Ralston)

JRD Citroën T55 Wagon
Made to a smaller scale than the cars (around 1/55), this Citroën covered wagon can also be found in military guise, towing a tanker trailer.
Price guide: £100

Dinky Toys 535 Citroën 2CV
With minor variations, this model was in production between 1952 and 1963. In 1967 Dinky brought out a more sophisticated 'Super Detail' version of the 2CV.
Price guide: £100

Quiralu Mercedes-Benz 300SL
A model of the famous 'Gullwing' coupé which, in real life, had doors that hinged upwards. Like the other Quiralus, it was reissued in the 1990s, this time with window glazing.
Price guide: £150 (original); £15 (reissue)

Dinky Toys 24U Simca Aronde
Introduced in 1953, this model of the Aronde followed the evolution of the real car, and had a redesigned grille fitted in 1956. The two-tone finish was briefly available from 1958-59.
Price guide: £150

Dinky Toys 24C/522 Citroën DS 19
Introduced in 1956, the Citroën was fitted with window glazing two years later and remained in production until 1968.
Price guide: £150

Dinky Toys 24A Chrysler New Yorker Convertible
This Dinky convertible represents a 1955 model – the same year as the CIJ Chrysler Windsor. It was introduced in 1956, renumbered 520 in 1959, and deleted in 1961.
Price guide: £110

Dinky Toys 24K/528 Simca Vedette Chambord
The V8-engined Simca echoed American styling of the period. The Dinky model was produced between 1959 and 1961.
Price guide: £100

FRANCE

Dinky Toys 560 Citroën 2CV Van 'Postes'
First produced as a red fire van, this yellow postal van was in the Dinky range from 1963-1970. The postman and mail box are current products from Norev.
Price guide: £100

Dinky Toys 549 Borgward Isabella
By the time this model of the German Borgward coupé was introduced in 1959, French Dinky Toys were being fitted with windows, interiors and suspension.
Price guide: £90

Dinky Toys 577 Berliet GAK Cattle Truck
One of several models on the Berliet GAK chassis, this cattle truck (or 'Bétaillère' in French) made much use of plastic in its construction. The cows are plastic, too!
Price guide: £150

Dinky Toys 586 Citroën P55 Camion Laitier
An extremely attractive model, the Citroën is very hard to find complete with its load of thirty plastic milk crates. It was in production between 1961 and 1965.
Price guide: £250

Dinky Toys 587 Citroën 1200kg Van Philips
This was an original choice of subject, based on a travelling showroom that demonstrated Philips household appliances in rural France. Both the side and rear doors open, and there is a transparent plastic roof section. Produced between 1964 and 1970.
Price guide: £300

Dinky Toys 1435 Citroën Presidentielle
One of the most sought-after French Dinky model, this Citroën is based on a vehicle originally built for President de Gaulle. It has numerous features, such as electric interior lighting, 'cloth' effect seats, and opening boot. It was in production for about a year, from 1970-71.
Price guide: £400

Dinky Toys 1404 Citroën ID 19 'Radio Luxembourg'
Another very desirable model from the last phase of French Dinky production, this TV camera car can be found with 'Radio Télé Luxembourg' or 'RTL Luxembourg' lettering on the door panels.
Price guide: £350+

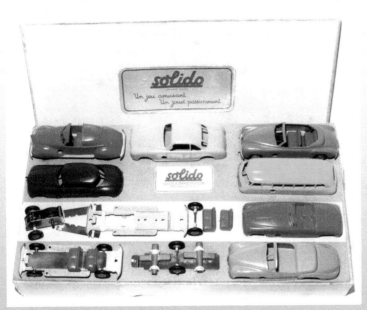

Solido Junior set
The idea behind the Solido 'Junior' series was to provide a selection of alternative bodies that could be fitted to a common chassis powered by a clockwork motor. Each vehicle was named after a French town and the selection in this boxed set comprises (clockwise from left): Loraine (believed to be a Chevrolet), Normandie (possibly a Matford), Alençon (Ford Comète), Cannes (Alfa Romeo), a Provence coach, Bourgogne (Ferrari) and Antibes (Delahaye). These were larger than 1/43 scale.
Price guide: £600+
(Courtesy Bruce Sterling)

FRANCE

Solido Junior Series cars
(Left-to-right, clockwise): Mercedes-Benz 300 (ref194), Cadillac ('Vichy') ref 90 and Ford Thunderbird (ref195). The earliest of the three is the Cadillac, which has a hole in the side door for the key. The Mercedes comes with or without a horizontally-mounted mechanism, operated by a key inserted underneath, whereas the Thunderbird is not motorised.
Price guide: £150+ each
(Courtesy Bruce Sterling)

Solido Peugeot 403 Cabriolet
Like all of the Solido convertibles, the Peugeot is rare in mint condition as the windscreen is easily broken.
Price guide: £100

Solido 100 Jaguar D Type and 107 Aston Martin
In 1957 Solido launched the 1/43 scale 100 series, concentrating on sports and racing cars. Britain was a significant force in motor racing in those days, hence the choice of Aston Martin DBR and Jaguar D Type.
Price guide: £80 each
(Courtesy David G Ralston)

Solido 115 Rolls-Royce Silver Cloud
Perhaps the most realistic model in the 100 series, the Silver Cloud captures the dignified lines of the original and is well-finished in a lacquered two-tone brown and metallic grey.
Price guide: £150

France Jouets Berliet Stradair
France Jouets made many variations on the Berliet GAK and Stradair chassis. This promotional model for Pierval, a brand of mineral water, is particularly rare. The presence of any paperwork that accompanied a toy, such as an instruction leaflet or, as in this case, an advertising booklet, will greatly add to its value on the collectors' market.
Price guide: £100

Les Rouliers
The Matchbox concept was as popular in France as in the UK. The small-scale Les Rouliers series is made up entirely of trucks and road-building equipment.
Price guide: £30 each

Gitanes
The packaging of the Gitanes series is even closer in style to Matchbox. Only ten different castings were made, the rarest being the Citroën DS 19. Pictured here are two Renaults; the Dauphine and the 1000kg van.
Price guide: £40 each

Majorette
By far the most successful small-scale French diecast brand is Majorette, still very popular today.
Left: Citroën GS. Right: Renault 5.
Price guide: £20 each

GERMANY

At the turn of the twentieth century, Germany was unchallenged as the European centre of toy production. In particular, the city of Nuremberg, which had a tradition of wooden toy manufacture stretching back as far as the fourteenth century, became famous for the production of tinplate toys, especially cars and trains. In 1905 the city boasted the world's biggest toy factory, Gebrüder Bing AG, employing approximately 2700 workers. Even today, the world's most important toy trade fair is held in Nuremberg.

Märklin

Some 85 miles away, in the town of Goppingen, a tinsmith by the name of Theodor Märklin started to make dolls' house accessories in 1859. It was largely as a result of his wife's business skills and determination that the enterprise survived after the death of the founder in 1866, and later prospered under one of his sons. In the 1890s Märklin launched a clockwork toy train system, and after the First World War pioneered electric trains. By 1935 a smaller OO gauge railway system had been launched and zinc diecasting was used for some components instead of tinplate. Märklin also acted as Meccano Limited's German distributor in the early 1930s and quickly adapted the Dinky Toy concept to the home market, bringing out some models of interesting German cars of the period, such as a Hanomag, an Adler and a Horch, together with some Auto Union and Mercedes racers. Most sought-after of all are the KdF Wagen (Volkswagen) and the Mercedes open limousine as used by Adolf Hitler.

After the war, Märklin introduced a new range of models, the first being a 1949 Buick Special, chosen, perhaps, as American cars would have been familiar in Germany during the period of the occupation. However, this was not typical of the rest of the range, which was made up exclusively of German vehicles once production of new models got going in the 1950s. These included the Mercedes 300 'Adenauer,' BMW 501 (issued in as many as ten colour variations), the Porsche 356, Ford Taunus 15M and 17M, BMW 507 coupé, Borgward Isabella and, of course, the Volkswagen Beetle. From 1957 existing models and all subsequent releases carried a four-figure reference number beginning with eight, which has led to the range becoming known as the Märklin 8000 series. All of these models are notable for the fine detail found on the castings.

Largely based on 1950s prototypes, the 8000 series was looking dated by the mid-sixties, and in 1968 Märklin launched a new 1800 range, with interiors, windows and opening parts. Only a couple of years later this series was renamed 'RAK' and fitted with high-speed wheels similar to Corgi's 'Whizzwheels' and Dinky's 'Speedwheels.' Once again, most of the models were based on German cars, with a preference for upmarket saloons (Mercedes-Benz 250, Audi 100, BMW 2500), and sporty coupés (BMW 1600 GT, Ford Capri). Manufacture was subcontracted to Mercury of Italy, a company whose connections with Märklin date back to before the Second World War.

When Mercury went out of business a few years later, Märklin diecasts production ceased.

Schuco

Founded in Nuremberg in 1912, Schreyer and Co gained a reputation for making toys with ingenious clockwork mechanisms, thanks to the inventiveness of co-founder Heinrich Müller. For example, the famous 'Examico' car of 1938, based on a prewar BMW, had a four-speed and reverse gearbox, while the 'Miraco' car could run along a table top and quickly turn as soon as it reached the edge. These toys had tinplate bodies, but in the 1950s Schuco adapted its clever mechanisms to fit diecast models in the Micro Racer series. Small

Pages from the 1959/60 Schuco catalogue. The Micro Racer series consisted of clockwork-powered cars in 1/40-1/50 scale, while the Schuco Piccolos were solid castings in 1/90 scale.

clockwork cars already existed, of course, but with the Schucos it was possible to disengage the clockwork mechanism and 'freewheel' the car, while rotating the exhaust pipe adjusted the steering. Packing all this into a Dinky-size car inevitably meant that realism had to take second place to ingenuity. Thus, the Micro Racer racing cars are somewhat caricatured but some of the others, like the Porsche 356, Mercedes 190SL and 220, Volkswagen and Ford Fairlane are reasonable likenesses. Like many of the Schuco tin toys, the Micro Racers have been remanufactured in China and are still distributed under the Schuco name today.

Prämeta

Still more mechanical ingenuity was incorporated into a small group of cars made in Cologne by Prämeta in the early fifties. According to the noted toy historian Mike Richardson, Prämeta is an amalgamation of the words 'Prämie,' meaning prize or award, and 'Metall.' The first model was a Volkswagen Beetle, later followed by a 1947 Buick Roadmaster, 1951 Mercedes 300, 1951 Jaguar XK 120 Coupé and 1953 Opel Kapitän. A key shaped liked the figure of a traffic policeman could be inserted underneath the car in order to operate a complex mechanism which allowed it to move either in a straight line or to make a series of turns. To hide the mechanism, the bodies had no window openings and came in either painted or chrome-plated finish. Of necessity, they were rather larger than 1/43 scale.

Gama

While the Schuco and Prämeta cars were an impressive attempt to marry the traditional German clockwork toy to the more modern diecast concept, they were expensive to produce. Hence, another long-established toy company, Gama, seized the opportunity to enter the market.

Gama was founded in 1882 by Georg Adam Mangold in Fürth and had already shown itself quick to move with the times, which is perhaps why it outlasted other famous Germany toy companies like Distler, JNF, Arnold and Tipp and Co. For example, Gama was one of the first to relinquish tinplate in favour of plastic as a raw material for its large-scale, friction-powered cars. In 1959 Gama launched the 1/43 Mini-Mod series, the first three models being the Ford Taunus, Opel Rekord and Volkswagen. In comparison to other European brands like Tekno of Denmark they were on the crude side but were no doubt cheaper and better distributed in Germany so that the range caught on quickly.

Among the most interesting Gamas were two small BMWs: the 600, an elongated four-seater version of the Isetta Bubble Car, and the more elegant 700 coupé designed by Michelotti. One German car of this period that found its way into almost every major diecast range was the Mercedes 220, and it was only to be expected that Gama would model this one, as it was a good base for taxi and police variations.

Gama also made numerous trucks, most of them based on three different chassis designs by Faun, Krupp and Mercedes, and a series of light commercials on a Volkswagen chassis. The pick-up was adapted into an extending ladder truck, the minibus became an

A selection of cars from a c.1960 Gama catalogue. The Lloyd Arabella pictured at the top of the page does not seem to have reached the production stage.

ambulance, and the van was issued in several liveries, such as 'Shell' and 'Aral.' These gave way to a second generation of VW Transporter vans in 1968, a long-lived casting that was still being made in the 1980s.

Influenced by the success of Matchbox Models of Yesteryear, Gama launched the 'Oldtimers' series in 1964 starting with a Benz 'vis-à-vis' and a Benz Victoria from 1893. During the next ten years a total of fourteen different subjects were modelled, and some remained in the Gama catalogue as late as 1984.

Siku

In previous chapters we have seen how the success of Matchbox toys in the 1960s increasingly forced other manufacturers to diversify into smaller scale diecasts. The Siku company had started making small HO scale cars before Matchbox, but these were plastic rather than

Die SIKU-Flitzer

sie sausen · they do run

V 283 Ford 20 M

V 296 Ford GT 40

V 285 Porsche Carrera 906

V 295 Maserati Mistral

V 304 Opel GT

V 302 Mercedes 280 SL

V 294 Jaguar E 2 + 2

V 271 Opel Rekord Coupé

V 266 BMW 2000 CS

natürliche Größe
natural size · grandeur nature
natuurlijke grootte · tamaño natural
grandezza naturale

A selection of 1/60 diecast cars from Siku's 1971 catalogue.

metal, as indicated by the name which stands for 'Sieper Kunststoff' – 'Sieper' being the name of the founder and 'Kunststoff' the German for plastic. In 1963 Siku recognised that a change to diecast metal was essential, and invested heavily in a new range of 1/60 scale models at its factory in Ludenscheidt – though these were not Siku's first metal products as the manufacture of the three-pointed star bonnet emblem for Mercedes-Benz cars had been subcontracted to the company in the early 1950s.

The new Siku metal cars were shown to the toy trade in January 1963. The first eight issues, as depicted in Siku's catalogue for that year, were a Fiat 1800, BMW 1500, Ford 12M, Opel Kadett, Cadillac Fleetwood, Volkswagen Microbus, Volkswagen Police bus with loudspeakers and a Porsche tractor, all of them priced at 1.50 DM compared to the 1.00 DM that was charged for most of the plastic cars. They caught on so quickly that in the next five years the range had expanded to as many as 68 models. Like the rest of the toy industry, Siku was affected by the huge success of Hot Wheels and had to follow suit by fitting low-friction wheels ('Siku-Flitzern'). Siku has been fortunate to survive the ups and downs of recent decades and continues to offer a range of well-made and reasonably-priced cars today.

Schuco Piccolo

A rather unusual entry into the small-scale diecast market was the Schuco Piccolo series of 1957. These little 1/90 scale models were made from solid metal castings with the windows picked out in silver paint. Their weight, combined with the tiny rubber tyres, meant that they could roll along a flat surface at some speed.

The first group comprised simple open racing cars, followed by

sports and saloon cars, mostly based on German prototypes like the Mercedes 190SL, Mercedes 220, VW Karmann Ghia and VW Beetle. There was, however, a sprinkling of other European cars too: an Austin-Healey, an MGA, a Citroën DS 19 and a Volvo PV 544. The appeal of the models is based on their charm rather than on accuracy, and some are certainly less realistic than others. On the other hand, some of the commercial vehicles were quite complicated, the most ambitious being a Coles lorry-mounted crane with numerous removable sections allowing the crane jib to extend to a height of more than ten inches.

By 1969 Schuco had started to phase out the Piccolo range in favour of a new 1/66 'Superschnell' series of diecast models of German cars, to be joined in 1973 by a 1/43 series. Both ranges featured the opening doors and low-friction wheels that appealed to children at the time. But the market was growing ever more competitive, and things became more difficult after founder Heinrich Müller died in 1974. By 1980 long-standing rival Gama had taken over the Schuco name.

Meanwhile, Schuco Piccolos were becoming increasingly sought-after on the collectors' market, and in 1994 they made a comeback. The range has now taken on a momentum of its own, and new models are being introduced that were not in the original line-up, with the manufacturer creating desirability by issuing many limited editions.

Other brands

As in other countries, many smaller brands made diecast cars in Germany. Some had little impact, such as Rex, which issued an Opel Kapitan and Ford Thunderbird in 1959-60. However, a company called Wittek, based in Lintorf, near Düsseldorf, produced a fairly extensive series of diecasts under the name RW Modell from 1963 until the mid-1970s. Many were light commercial vehicles: a Hanomag with a variety of bodies, a Ford Transit van in 'Aral,' 'BP' and Bundespost liveries, plus some diggers and forklift trucks. There were only four modern cars but these will certainly interest any collector of German vehicles of the period. Three were Opels – a 1971 Rekord, Commodore Coupé and a 1976 Manta – and may have been sold as promotional models, while the other was a Mercedes-Benz 600 limousine in short wheelbase form, unlike the Dinky and Corgi models which were based on the longer Pullman version. Wittek also made veteran and vintage cars sold under the name Ziss. The range included some unusual vehicles, such as the 1906 Adler, 1924 Hanomag Roadster, and BMW Dixi, along with the inevitable Model T Fords.

Märklin 8021 Volkswagen Karmann Ghia
Smaller than the equivalent Dinky Toys version, this simple model of the VW Beetle-based Karmann Ghia is typical of the style of the Märklin 8000 series.
Price guide: £150

Märklin 8020 Borgward Isabella
Like others in the series, the Borgward saloon can be found in numerous colours, some of them two-tone.
Price guide: £150

Märklin 8007 Volkswagen Van 'Gasolin'
In contrast to the Danish Tekno model, the Märklin Volkswagen T1 delivery van was not issued in many advertising liveries. This 'Gasolin' van was the standard issue, though two extremely rare promotionals ('Der Spiegel' and 'Sillan') also exist.
Price guide: £200

Märklin 8003 Mercedes-Benz 300
The 300 was a favourite of the German Chancellor Adenauer and makes for an imposing diecast model.
Price guide: £150
(Courtesy David G Ralston)

Märklin 8017 Phoenix Van 'Firestone'
This unusual van has opening doors at the rear made from tinplate. The three-tone colour scheme must have involved several spraying operations.
Price guide: £200

Schuco 713 Piccolo Mercedes 190SL
The 1/90 scale Piccolos are small but heavy, being cast in solid metal. The 190SL was originally issued between 1962 and 1969, but a reissue appeared in 1996.
Price guide: £50

Schuco Piccolo 750 Krupp Tipper
Introduced in 1958, this Krupp chassis formed the basis of several different Schuco Piccolo commercial vehicles, the largest being a car transporter capable of carrying six cars.
Price guide: £60

Prämeta
Three of the five mechanical cars issued by Prämeta, showing the various finishes: (left-to-right) two-tone Opel Kapitan, plated Jaguar XK 120, and cream-painted Buick.
Price guide: £300 each
(Courtesy Bruce Sterling)

GERMANY

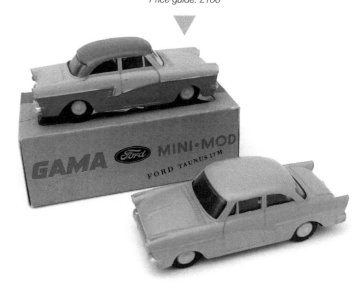

Prämeta Opel Kapitan
Another view of the Opel, showing the policeman -shaped key. The cutaway model on the left is thought to have been supplied to toy shops in order to demonstrate the ingenious mechanism.
Price guide: £300 each
(Courtesy Bruce Sterling)

Gama 901 Ford Taunus
Introduced in 1957, the Taunus 17M looked like a scaled-down American car of the period. Although not as detailed as the Märklins, Gama models had window glazing and tended to be finished in brighter colours.
Price guide: £100

Gama 902 Opel Rekord
The Rekord was General Motors' entry into the same mid-range family car market as the Taunus. Early Gama issues had white plastic wheels, later replaced by 'chrome' hubs.
Price guide: £100

Gama 908 Volkswagen ADAC
This Volkswagen is in the livery of the Allgemeiner Deutscher Automobil-Club (ADAC) which provides roadside assistance for motorists in Germany. Other liveries include 'Deutsche Bundespost,' 'Feuerwehr' and 'Polizei.'
Price guide: £80

Gama 9130 Buick
Most Gamas represent German vehicles, an exception being this 1959 Buick Electra, which is also available in metallic light blue with a white roof.
Price guide: £80

Gama 947 BMW 2000CS Coupé
Like Dinky, Corgi and other makes, Gamas gradually appeared with opening parts. Note the 'pillarless' side window arrangement.
Price guide: £60
(Courtesy David G Ralston)

Gama 9490 Volkswagen 1500
The slightly matte paint finish on this VW 1500 is typical of Gamas of the period.
Price guide: £60

Gama 9355 Mercedes-Benz 220S Taxi
Another Gama model which served as the base for numerous variations. This taxi features a roof sign and aerial, and also comes in black.
Price guide: £60

Gama 942 DKW F102
The F102 was the last car to bear the DKW badge. After 1965 DKW passed into Volkswagen ownership and the car re-emerged under the Audi name. The bonnet opens on this Gama version.
Price guide: £60

Gama 950 Volkswagen Van 'Shell'
The Volkswagen TI delivery has been much modelled in different European countries. The Gama also comes as a minibus with windows, and as a pick-up, crane truck, and Coca-Cola delivery truck.
Price guide: £100

Gama 911 Breakdown Truck
Gama used the same chassis as the basis for numerous commercial vehicles, though these do not seem to be as popular with collectors as the cars.
Price guide: £40

Gama 9518 Volkswagen Vans
In 1967 Volkswagen updated its van and Gama followed suit. The 'Esso' livery is a standard issue, but the other model is a much rarer promotional vehicle in the livery of a service van used by Lansing fork lift trucks.
Price guide: £30 ('Esso'); £70 ('Lansing')

Siku V230 Volkswagen

Well-known as a producer of 1/60th plastic cars since the mid-1950s, Siku launched a new diecast series in the same scale in 1963. Inevitably, a Volkswagen Beetle was included in the range.
Price guide: £40

Siku V211 Volkswagen Microbus

Volkswagen's minibus was almost as popular in model form and replicas of it are still produced today. The Siku also came in a dark green police livery.
Price guide: £50

Siku V244 Mercedes-Benz 250SE Taxi

Available as a plain saloon car in light blue (V256), the Mercedes was also issued in this taxi livery.
Price guide: £50

Siku V220 Tempo Matador

The Tempo Matador minibus is not as well-known as the Volkswagen. The Siku model has a sliding side door and a roof rack with canoe and paddles, which are easily lost.
Price guide: £70

SPAIN & ITALY

Between 1905 and 1936 at least three major manufacturers of toy cars were active in Spain: Paya, Rico, and Jyesa, all based in the town of Ibi near the Costa Blanca. Ibi was Spain's 'toy town,' just as Nuremberg was Germany's. However, these toys were made from tinplate and, later, plastic. A candidate for the title of the first genuinely Spanish diecast model would be the Seat 1400 by Jadali. Both the box and the underside of the model identify the maker as Metamol, based – like Seat – in Barcelona.

Metamol must have had considerable expertise in diecast mould making, for it got it right first time and the Seat is every bit as good as any other diecast of the mid-fifties. It's very Dinky-like in construction, with white tyres and tin base riveted to the body, but it is rather larger, being nearly five inches in length. However, it seems that this is the one and only diecast car that Jadali ever made, although it was issued in a number of varieties: a black and yellow Barcelona taxi; a black and red Madrid taxi; a black police car; and a white ambulance car with a red cross. All are extremely rare.

Dalia

Jadali may have intended the Seat to be the first in a series of Spanish diecasts but for one reason or another it was not to be. That honour belongs to another firm, Dalia, which had been licensed to produce French Solido toys in Spain since the early 1930s. Solido had pioneered the 'Autos Transformables' concept, by which a common chassis could be fitted with several different bodies and the Spanish issues were more or less identical to the French ones. The link with Solido was to continue but Dalia took an eclectic approach and in 1957 turned to Mercury of Italy for the tooling to make models of motor scooters in 1/32 scale. In those days, before mass car ownership, scooters were far more widely used in countries like Spain and Italy than today, not just for personal transport or with sidecars, but as light delivery vehicles. The two popular models of the period, Lambretta and Vespa, were both made by Dalia as scooters with or without sidecars, and there were also tricycles with a cargo-carrying bay at the front (known as 'motocarros'), supplied complete with loads like crates of bottles or butane gas containers.

It was to 1/43 scale cars that Dalia next turned its attention. When Solido introduced the 100 series fitted with spring suspension, this range was produced in Spain too, though colour schemes were sometimes different and later issues were often decorated with transfers that did not appear on their French counterparts. Only one Dalia car was an original casting – a Seat 1400C, later designated as a 1500 to reflect an increase in the car's engine size. Other Solido-based products were marked 'Dalia-Solido' underneath, but the Seat has the Dalia name alone, though there is still a close family resemblance and the car is fitted with Solido's patented spring suspension.

Dalia got further mileage out of the casting by issuing taxis (black/yellow for Barcelona and black/red for Madrid). Other variations include a black police car and a silver version carrying transfers on the front doors depicting the logo of the Spanish airline 'Iberia.'

Diecast expansion

With the expansion in Spain's car industry from the late 1960s onwards, thanks to links with car makers in other countries – Fiat at first, but others later, notably Ford – a parallel process occurred in the miniature car industry. A host of Spanish diecast car ranges appeared, most of them using tooling bought from or licensed by more established companies, such as Dinky, Corgi, Tekno, Mebetoys and Politoys. From having hardly any indigenous diecasts to speak of, the market in Spain was suddenly crowded by competing products from the likes of Joal, Pilen, Guisval and many others.

Because these companies all relied to a greater or lesser extent on tooling bought from other sources, many of the models seem vaguely familiar. Moreover, similar subjects were frequently duplicated, so that it's sometimes difficult to distinguish between the various ranges. As a listing of all Spanish diecasts would fill many pages only a general survey can be provided here.

Joal

To British collectors, Joal is perhaps the most familiar Spanish diecast range, as the company is still going strong today, now specialising in models of construction equipment. Although formed in the late 1940s to manufacture locksmiths' fittings as well as some metal toys, notably

The first item in the Joal range was a Jaguar E Type, based on a Danish Tekno model.

guns, Joal branched into 1/43 scale diecast cars around 1968, using moulds from various companies, especially Tekno of Denmark. The Mercedes 300SL and 230SL sports, Chevrolet Monza and Jaguar E Type had all first appeared in the Tekno catalogue. However, the fit of the opening parts was not quite as good on the Spanish issues, and the paint finish tended to be rather thick.

A couple of long-running British Dinkies found their way to Spain as well: the Albion Cement Mixer and the Blaw Knox Bulldozer, though there is some debate about whether these are copies or made from the original moulds. The tooling for some Italian Fiat models also provided an easy way for Joal to add some Seats to its lineup.

Among Joal's original designs were various Pegaso trucks. While other manufacturers often combined metal and plastic construction, the Joal trucks are all metal, giving them a heavy feel. A catalogue from 1979 shows the original models of ten years earlier still in production, having been joined by some more recent cars like the Citroën SM, CX and Ford Fiesta, while the selection of Caterpillar construction equipment is an indication of the direction in which Joal was to move in future.

Pilen

Joal quickly found competition from another Spanish diecast range produced in Ibi: Auto Pilen, later known simply as Pilen.

Pilen's first venture into diecast was a range of formula one racing cars in 1/41 scale, but from 1969 onwards Joal and Pilen competed head-on with similar 1/43 scale cars, again using old tooling: the Chevrolet Corvette, for example, came from Corgi, and the Mercedes 250 from Mebetoys of Italy.

The most significant thing about Pilen, though, is the Dinky connection. By the early 1970s French Dinky was in grave difficulties and production ceased at the factory in Bobigny on the outskirts of Paris. The Dinky name was a valuable asset, though, and in 1974 moulds for several French Dinky cars were transferred to Pilen which marketed them as Dinky Toys made in Spain. There were various minor casting changes and different colour schemes, and details of these can be found in Jean-Michel Roulet's *Histoire des Dinky Toys Français*. Finally, another group of original Pilen models was issued under the Dinky name. Ironically, this Spanish toy maker that had at first depended on moulds from other European companies ended up supporting French Dinky, if only for a few years.

Compared to French Dinkies, the Spanish issues were undervalued by collectors during the eighties and nineties, and prices were low. Now, though, they are considerably more expensive. The most desirable issue is undoubtedly the Citroën DS 23, a reworking of the earlier French Dinky Citroën DS 19 (Ref. 530) with the later style of headlights.

Nacoral Intercars

Unlike most other Spanish toy companies, this range was not made in Ibi but in a factory at Zaragoza. Dating from 1967, the first series, known as 'Chiqui Cars,' was in plastic, but some were also made in metal, paving the way for the 'Intercars' range which appeared around 1973. Some of these used tooling from the Belgian Sablon range, but Nacoral soon started to produce its own diecast models, among them several Volvos – the 144 and 244 DL, the 145 estate – and a Saab 99 Combi.

Mira

A later arrival on the Spanish diecast scene was Mira who, in the mid-seventies, launched a series of 1/64 Pegaso trucks, later joined by eight 1/43 cars: Ford Fiesta, VW Scirocco, Mercedes 450 SE, Chrysler 150 (Alpine), Citroën CX 2400, Seat 128 Coupé, Seat 1200 Coupé, and Seat 131. Mira managed to make eight models go further by

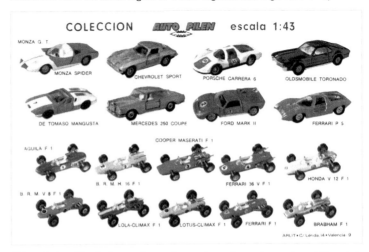

This early Auto Pilen leaflet reveals a preference for exotic sports coupés and Formula 1 racing cars.

producing all kinds of police, taxi, ambulance, fire and rally variations, though the Sciroccos with *The Saint* logo and in *Starsky and Hutch* colours were a bit far-fetched! Today, Mira is still a big player in the diecast field, now specialising in 1/18 and 1/25 scale classic American cars.

Guisval

Guisval was founded in Ibi in 1962 and is still producing toys today. While most Guisval products have been in the toy rather than the model category, some are of interest to the collector.

In the seventies, a few cars were made to the rather unusual scale of 1/37, the Ford Capri being the one to look out for. It can be found in police, ski club and rally variations. In the eighties there were quite a few 1/43 models – among them a Ford Sierra, Renault Espace, and BMW 325i – but they had unsightly wheels and were covered in garish stickers. The 1/30 scale Mercedes 300 SL and 1957 Ford Thunderbird were rather better.

As well as a long-running series of vintage and classic cars, Guisval currently makes some reasonable models of the Mercedes A Class, Citroën 2CV and Seat 600, while the Volkswagen New Beetle is considerably better finished than many of its other cars.

Italy

In some ways the development of the diecast car industry in Italy was similar to that in Spain: the market was dominated by one make, Mercury, for many years until the mid-1960s when numerous competitors emerged. As in Spain, there was a certain amount of overlap between the types of car modelled by companies such as Politoys, Mebetoys and Edil Toys.

Mercury

Founded in Turin in 1932, Mercury originally made diecast components for other companies. Its first metal toy was a gun, introduced in 1939, although prior to that the company already had an involvement in the toy industry as it acted as the Italian importer of German Märklin toys – a connection that was maintained into the 1970s, when Märklin distributed some Mercury cars in Germany.

A small book by M Batazzi published many years ago, entitled *Storia della Mercury 1945-1962* describes how Mercury began making toy cars after the end of the second World War by taking photos and making sketches of cars spotted at the Pininfarina coachworks, which was in the same industrial zone of Turin as the Mercury factory. As these early models, in around 1/40 scale, were not based on factory plans, they tended to be rather inaccurate likenesses, and were given vague names such as the 'Aero' coupé and 'Americana' sedan. More easily identifiable Italian and American subjects followed: Lancia Aprilia, Lincoln Continental convertible, Cadillac and Studebaker Commander. There were also a number of Italian and German racing cars, while the introduction of a 1949 Fiat Topolino and a 1950 Fiat 1400 saloon signalled an interest in modelling the kind of cars that were starting to appear on Italian roads at the time.

Many other popular Italian cars were made in a smaller 1/45 scale, starting with a 1953 Fiat 1100. To many collectors this series,

Mercury was one of the first to make diecast models with opening doors, bonnets and boots. This catalogue dates from the early 1960s.

issued between 1954 and 1961, represents Mercury's finest period. With their slightly smaller dimensions, chromed wheel hubs and light grey or black plastic tyres, and distinctive blue and red packaging, these models have a unique character. While most were, naturally enough, based on contemporary Fiats, Lancia, Autobianchis and Alfa Romeos, there was also a Volkswagen Beetle, Studebaker Golden Hawk, Cadillac Eldorado convertible, and a Rolls-Royce Silver Cloud (also issued with a different radiator as a Bentley S Type). Also dating from this period were some small commercial vehicles, notably a Saurer box van and a Viberti tanker, both issued in a variety of liveries.

Mercury made a surprising leap forward in about 1964, not only adopting the standard 1/43 size but introducing a model of the Fiat 2300S on which the doors, bonnet and boot opened – sometimes claimed to be the first such model to combine all these features which

A rare Saurer furniture van as pictured in Mercury's 1959-60 catalogue.

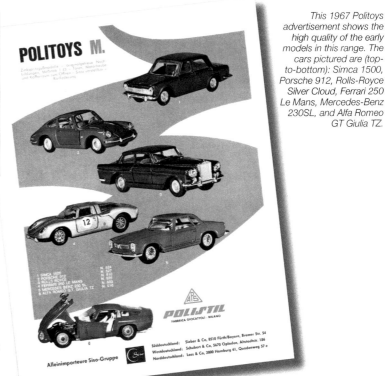

had earlier appeared separately on various Dinky and Corgi toys. This was followed by a Maserati 2500GT coupé with the same characteristics – and a set of golf clubs in the boot, too! Subsequent Mercury models maintained the sporty emphasis, such as the Lancia Flavia, Mercedes 230SL, and Ferrari 250 LM.

Dugu, Politoys and Mebetoys

While these were all good models, Mercury no longer had the Italian diecast market to itself. In 1962, Rio began to make vintage vehicles, many of which have remained in production for over thirty years. Soon afterwards, Dugu, based in Varallo Sesia in the Piedmont region, launched a range of models of veteran and vintage cars in the Museo dell'Automobile Carlo Biscaretti di Ruffia in Turin. Although this type of model is not so popular with collectors now, two Dugu issues appeal to American car enthusiasts (no. 13, the 1931 Duesenberg and no. 18, the 1936 Cord). The 1936 Fiat 500 (M8) and 1948 Cisitalia Coupé (M10) are also sought-after, perhaps because they are based on later prototypes than the typical Dugu product.

A more direct threat to Mercury came from Politoys which had been making an extensive range of plastic cars since 1960 in the somewhat unusual scale of 1/41. In 1965 Politoys diversified into diecast, and although many of the subjects chosen were already represented in other ranges, there were also some inspired choices, notably a Maserati Quattroporte (four doors), Volkswagen 1600 Station Wagon, Citroën DS 21, Ghia V280, and Jensen Interceptor. In an attempt to publicise its products, Politoys even became involved – albeit briefly – in the sponsorship of Formula One racing. As happened so often, cost-cutting led to a deterioration of the quality of the toys in the 1970s, by which time the name had been changed to Polistil to avoid confusion with the better known Palitoy company.

In 1967 yet another Italian diecast brand was launched: Mebetoys, short for 'Meccannica Besana Toys' after Mario Besana, the founder. The first in the series was a Fiat 850, followed by a Fiat 1500 and an Alfa Romeo Giulia TI – all modelled by others, but the fourth model – an Alfa Romeo 2600 – was a more original choice. In spite of the competition, Mebetoys managed to make its mark, and after issuing forty models the owner sold out to Mattel of the USA which continued to develop the brand, though later issues were more toys than models. The energetic Signor Besana then went on to found

Burago, famous for its 1/18 scale models. Early Mebetoys are sought-after by collectors today, and enthusiasts have set up a website (www.mebetoys.com) which traces the development of the range.

Catalogue of the Dugu range of veteran car models, which were based on vehicles exhibited in the Museo dell'Automobile Carlo Biscaretti di Ruffia in Turin.

SPAIN & ITALY

Mercury 10 Fiat 500C
An attractive early Mercury model based on the third generation Fiat Topolino, produced between 1949 and 1955.
Price guide: £90
(Courtesy Douglas R Kelly)

Mercury 94 Autocarro 'Ciclope'
A number of different body styles appeared on this truck chassis, including a crane, flat lorry and tipper.
Price guide: £90
(Courtesy Douglas R Kelly)

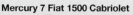

Mercury 9 Fiat 1500
The Fiat 1300/1500 range dates from 1961. By this period Mercury models had windows, suspension and interior fittings.
Price guide: £75

Mercury 7 Fiat 1500 Cabriolet
This convertible version of the 1500 came in a wide range of different colours and is harder to find than the saloon.
Price guide: £100

Mercury 14 Lancia Appia
Dating from 1953, the Appia was a small luxury saloon with doors that were hinged in an unusual way, which did away with the need for a central door pillar.
Price guide: £90

Mercury 15 Volkswagen
Mercury's version of the post-1953 oval window VW Beetle has been seen in at least six different colour schemes, in addition to a rare yellow/black Swiss PTT version.
Price guide: £100

Mercury 27 Studebaker Golden Hawk
The Studebaker was a popular choice for model manufacturers, including Dinky and Corgi in the UK. The Mercury is based on a 1957 model, and can be found in many two-tone colour combinations.
Price guide: £175
(Courtesy Gary Cohen)

Mercury 6 Autobianchi Bianchina
The Bianchina combined Fiat 500 mechanicals with a more stylish bodyshell. The Mercury model has windows but no interior fittings.
Price guide: £75

SPAIN & ITALY

Mercury 29 Alfa Romeo Cangura
This Alfa Romeo is typical of the exotic coupés which were a speciality of Mercury in the mid-1960s.
Price guide: £80
(Courtesy Douglas R Kelly)

Mercury Ferrari Gift Set
This rare 'Squadra Corse Ferrari' gift set contains one Ferrari 250 LM and four versions of the 330P, with a selection of spare wheels.
Price guide: £500+
(Courtesy Gary Cohen).

Dugu 8 Fiat 500A
Most Dugu models were based on cars of the late 19th and early 20th century, but the Fiat Topolino is based on a 1936 prototype.
Price guide: £50
(Courtesy Alex J Cameron)

Politoys 545 Citroën DS 21
One of the most sought-after Politoys is this Citroën, issued in 1969. The following year, less realistic plastic wheels were fitted, making the first issue more desirable.
Price guide: £100

Politoys 573 Jensen Vignale Coupé
There were few British subjects in the Politoys range. As with others in the series, the Jensen comes with two different wheel styles.
Price guide: £75
(Courtesy David G Ralston)

Politoys 567 Oldsmobile Toronado
The grille design on this model indicates that it is a representation of a 1967 Toronado, whereas the Corgi and Solido versions are based on a 1966 prototype.
Price guide: £90
(Courtesy Gary Cohen)

Polistil 34 Batmobile
Although the dimensions of the model are slightly larger, Polistil's interpretation of the Batmobile has many similarities to the better-known Corgi Toys item.
Price guide: £200
(Courtesy Gary Cohen)

Mebetoys A31 Mini Cooper Rallye
Based on the standard Mini issue (ref A 28), this Rallye model was issued between 1969 and 1974 with added spotlights and Monte Carlo rally decorations.
Price guide: £50
(Courtesy Gary Cohen)

Mebetoys A22 Chevrolet Corvette Rondine
The Corvette Rondine was an elegant concept car with coachwork by Pininfarina, and shown at the 1963 Paris Motor Show. The Mebetoys model appeared in 1966.
Price guide: £40
(Courtesy Gary Cohen)

Dalia Seat 1400C
Most Dalia cars were Solido and Tekno models issued under licence, but the Spanish Seat was an original casting. It also came as a taxi and with the logo of Iberia, the Spanish airline.
Price guide: £100-£200
(Courtesy Douglas R Kelly)

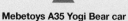

Mebetoys A35 Yogi Bear car
Produced between 1968 and 1973, this model came with figures of Yogi Bear and Boo Boo from the Hanna-Barbera animated cartoon series.
Price guide: £150
(Courtesy Gary Cohen)

Dalia 1463/6 Vespa with Sidecar
Dalia also made a large series of Vespa and Lambretta scooters in 1/32 scale, with and without sidecars.
Price guide: £60

Jadali Seat 1400
This very rare mid-1950s Seat is the only known diecast car made by Metamol and sold under the name Jadali.
Price guide: £300+
(Courtesy Juan Mauri Cruz)

Jadali Seat 1400
The Jadali can also be found in two-tone colours. Although very similar in construction to a Dinky Toy model, the item is slightly larger in scale, at nearly five inches long.
Price guide: £300+
(Courtesy Juan Mauri Cruz)

Jadali Seat 1400 Madrid Taxi
At the time the Jadali model was made, Madrid taxis were black with a red side stripe. Today, the city's taxis carry a less distinctive white livery.
Price guide: £300+
(Courtesy Juan Mauri Cruz)

Jadali Seat 1400 Barcelona Taxi
This black and yellow livery is still in used on Barcelona taxis today.
Price guide: £300+
(Courtesy Juan Mauri Cruz)

Joal 115 Iso Rivolta
This exotic Italian supercar, powered by a V8 Chevrolet engine, was built in limited numbers between 1962 and 1970. Doors, boot and bonnet open on the Joal model.
Price guide: £25

Pilen M-503 Citroën DS 23
Although it was issued in 1974 (which puts it outside the period covered by this book), Pilen's Citroën was in fact modified from the 1960s French Dinky Citroën DS 19 casting.
Price guide: £60

Pilen M-297 Mercedes 250 Taxi
The distinctive black and yellow livery of Barcelona's taxis has appeared on many Spanish models, though it is doubtful whether a two-door coupé would be used as a taxi in real life!
Price guide: £25

Joal 208 Pegaso Tanker
Joal made several different variations on this Pegaso truck. Unusually, the tank section is manufactured of metal rather than plastic, making for a very heavy model.
Price guide: £25

Denmark: Tekno

Denmark may not take up much space on a map of Europe but it made a very significant contribution to the development of diecast toys. Many collectors consider that the Danish Tekno series set a standard unequalled by any of its competitors in the 1950s and '60s.

Prior to the Second World War, most toys sold in Denmark came from Germany. Spotting a potential market for home-grown playthings, a plumber by the name of Andreas Siegumfeldt diversified into wooden and tinplate toys, with considerable success. In the mid-1930s Siegumfeldt offered a range of well-made Tekno tinplate trucks consisting of different body designs on the same cab/chassis base. Many were in the colours of 'Falck,' the Danish emergency service, and Tekno also made some elaborate wooden buildings to go with them.

It was the wartime shortage of tin that led Tekno to turn to diecasting, as the main raw material – zinc – was easier to obtain. Tekno had no experience in the field, but proved to be a quick learner, and was soon producing some of the finest 1/43 models in Europe. In its heyday, Tekno was turning out more than one million toy cars per year.

Tekno's early diecasts, such as the Buick ambulance and 1949 Mercury sedan, were not particularly realistic, but even at that stage the company was incorporating features like steering, simple interior fittings and even a sliding radio aerial. The choice of American vehicles reflects the significance of North America as an export market, and Tekno worked through importers based in Buffalo, NY, and Toronto. Some models were adapted for export: the Dodge beer truck, for example, was sold at home in the livery of Danish brewers Tuborg, whereas it carried 'Blue Ribbon Beer' for the American market.

High quality advertising decals were to be Tekno's hallmark. These, more than anything else, are what make a Tekno a Tekno. The company's skill in this area reached its climax in a magnificent series of

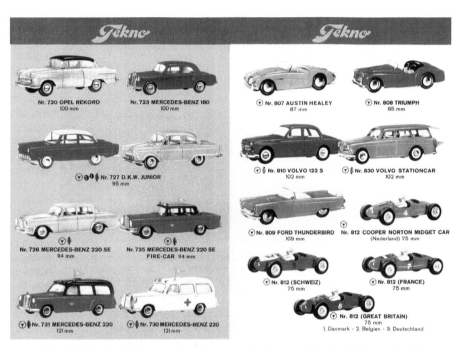

This mid-1960s Danish Tekno catalogue shows cars from Germany, Sweden, Britain and the USA.

Ford and Volkswagen delivery vans, of which more than 160 variations have been recorded. Some, like the green and white Ford Taunus for Stockmann's department store, were done as special orders, while others, like the more readily obtainable Volkswagen Philips van, were on general sale for some time.

Early Tekno cars varied in scale from 1/40 to 1/50, but Tekno eventually settled on the standard 1/43 size, modelling many interesting vehicles, like the Ford Thunderbird convertible, Lincoln Continental, Volvo PV544 and Amazon, numerous Mercedes ambulances, Saab 96, and lesser-known cars like the Lloyd from Germany.

By 1969, the company's finest days were over. The founder, Mr

By the end of the 1960s the Tekno range had been slimmed down, though there were still many interesting models. This scene from the 1970 catalogue includes (clockwise, from bottom left): 459 Volvo fire engine, 445 Scania 76 fire escape, 408 Volkswagen fire engine and ladder trailer, 835 Volvo 144 'Politi,' and 415 Ford Taunus Transit ambulance.

Sweden: Lemeco, Lenyko and Geno

In contrast to Denmark, only a few diecast cars were made in Sweden. For instance, in the early 1950s a small range called Lemeco was manufactured in Stockholm, containing a Ford Fordor and an Austin Devon, both of which look suspiciously like the Dinky versions. In April 1981 *Modellers' World* magazine related the story of how a toy wholesaler in Gothenburg by the name of Gösta Norën decided to market a model car, the locally-built Volvo PV444 being a natural choice. From 1958 onwards some 10,000 examples were made until a fire destroyed Gösta Norën's premises in 1963. These models can be found either with a base marked 'Geno' or with a plain silver base, packed in a grey box marked 'Lenyko.' The Volvo proved not only to be the first item in the Lenyko/Geno series but the last. It is rare today.

Holland: Lion Car and Best Box

After the Second World War Mr A van Leeuwen set up Lion Toys, specialising in making model railway track from scrap tinplate. Another ten years passed before the first diecast car – a Volkswagen Beetle – appeared. This was soon followed by a Renault 4CV, and although neither of these cars could claim to be particularly accurate replicas they certainly exhibit all the charm and simplicity of 1950s diecasts. Like the Dinky Toys items of the same period these early Lion cars had tinplate bases, although at first they were attached with screws rather than rivets – which makes life much easier for collectors who like to restore playworn examples.

The Volkswagen and Renault have always been popular in model form but the next two subjects were less obvious choices: a 1956 Opel Olympia Rekord and a DKW 3=6. The fifth and last non-Dutch saloon car to be modelled was a Renault Dauphine, which gained window glazing and interior fittings at a later stage of its production. After this, Lion Car shifted its emphasis to home-grown products. The reason was that in 1958 the first truly Dutch car for many years went on sale, the Daf 600, and it was natural that Holland's only major motor manufacturer would team up with the country's only significant diecast manufacturer. Hence, Lion Car's model of the original Daf closely followed the real car's evolution from the 600 through the Daffodil to the 33 and so on, right up to the 66, the last car to carry the Daf badge. The link was so close that instead of using a colour chart Daf dealers would show potential customers a selection of Lion cars sprayed in the correct colour schemes. Lion also made many different Daf trucks, and the manufacture of modern trucks under the Lion name continues to this day.

Lion Cars was not the only Dutch company to make model cars. In the late 1950s a new range, Best Box, was launched, clearly influenced by the Matchbox concept, and the first model in the range was also a Daf. This was followed by other European cars, such as a Jaguar E Type, Ford Taunus, Opel Rekord, and Citroën ID 19 Estate. Later, the name was changed to Efsi, and many different liveries appeared on a series of Model T Ford and Citroën vans, and on other commercial vehicles.

Siegumfeldt, died that year and his family had no particular interest in continuing the business. However, after some years of difficulty, Tekno production recommenced in Holland in 1972, and today the company specialises in model trucks in the liveries of European haulage companies.

As far as most collectors are concerned, the entire history of the Danish model car industry begins and ends with Tekno. However, a book published in 2002 by Danish toy experts Dorte Johansen and Hans Hedegård brought to light many other small brands with unfamiliar names like BP, Blue Sun, Joker Bilen, Stentorp, and Tobi Toys. Some of these are copies of Tekno and other products, often in plastic. A more extensive diecast range was offered by Vilmer, active in Kalundborg between approximately 1952 and 1965. Early Vilmer commercial vehicles were similar to Teknos, but later more original trucks were issued with Chevrolet, Volvo, Bedford, and Ford Thames Trader cabs. Vilmer also made four extremely rare cars: a Renault 4CV, Opel Rekord estate, Volvo 444, and Mercedes 180.

Belgium: Gasquy and Sablon

Very little is known about the history of the Gasquy-Septoy brand, except that production dates from the late 1940s. This range falls into two distinct categories: the best and the rest! The racing car, trucks, Buick coupé and bus are crude likenesses, whereas three other American cars – a 1949 Ford, Studebaker and Chevrolet are in a completely different league. The most sought-after Gasquy, however, is the rear-engined Czechoslovakian Tatra T600, a car which has something of a cult following.

It was not until 1968 that another Belgian company ventured into the diecast field: Sablon[1], which negotiated a deal with a local chocolate factory, 'Jacques,' which used the models as part of a promotion. There were nine models in the series: a Porsche 911, Mercedes-Benz 250SE, Renault 16, BMW 2000CS, BMW 1600, Lamborghini Marzal, NSU Ro80, BMW 1600GT, and Glas 3000 V8 coupé. The castings were up to the standard of the competition and had plenty of opening parts, but the models were clearly not original enough to find a niche, and production lasted for only a couple of years. Moreover, the series suffered from a fatal flaw: a chemical reaction occured between the material used for the tyres and the wheel hubs, meaning that surviving models have misshapen wheels.

Portugal: Metosul

Luso Celulóide was founded in the 1940s by the Henriques Brothers in Espinho near Oporto, and made various plastic products, including toy cars. The company's name was reversed to produce the trademark 'Osul.' Then in 1965 came Metosul which, as the name implies, was a series of cars made from diecast metal. These were derived from models in several other European ranges, and it may well be that Luso bought redundant tooling from the manufacturers. The Alfa Romeo Giulietta Spider, for example, is very similar to the French Solido version, the Mercedes-Benz 200 comes from the German Gama range, the Renault Floride and Citroën DS resemble Corgi Toys items, and the Leyland Atlantean bus is very like the Dinky Toys model – although the entry doors appear on the opposite side as it is left-hand drive. Metosuls were still in production in the late 1980s, and were, for a long time, undervalued; collectors are now taking notice of them and prices are rising.

Although based on 1960s models originally made by other manufacturers, the Portuguese Metosul range was still in production in the 1980s.

3 Alfa Romeo Giulietta Spyder	2 Citroen DS 19
1 Renault Floride	4 Volkswagen

[1] The story of the Sablon range has been traced in detail in an article by Mike Richardson in Model Collector magazine, September 1991.

OTHER EUROPEAN COUNTRIES

Tekno 429 Mercury
The first two diecast cars modelled by Tekno were both American; a 1947 Ford and this 1949 Mercury, which incorporated some advanced features for its time, such as interior fittings and a sliding radio aerial.
Price guide: £150

Tekno 804 MG Midget
The early fifties were the golden age of British sports cars, and four of these were modelled by Tekno – a Jaguar XK 120, a Triumph TR2, an Austin-Healey, and this 1952 MG TD.
Price guide: £100

Tekno 719 Morris Oxford
Whitewall tyres, window glazing, clear plastic headlamp lenses, separate bumpers and chrome grille are typical of Tekno's attention to detail. The box illustration makes effective use of a period sales brochure.
Price guide: £100

Tekno 811 Renault 4CV
An excellent replica of a 1955 Renault 4CV. Note the box style, which depicts different Renault cars on each face, even though these were not modelled by Tekno.
Price guide: £125

Tekno 817 Lloyd Stationcar
The Lloyd was a small German car of the 1950s, modelled by Tekno in saloon, estate car and van forms.
Price guide: £100

Tekno 819 Volkswagen 1200
No. 805 in the Tekno range was a 1953 oval window Beetle, but this was replaced by a new casting representing a 1957 model which remained in production for many years. Variations include Danish, German and Swiss postal cars, several police cars, and even Herbie from the Walt Disney film!
Price guide: £100

Tekno 822 Volvo PV544
The PV544 was an updated version of the earlier PV444 which dates back to 1944. The Tekno is based on a 1959 model.
Price guide: £150

Tekno 828 VW 1500
Like the Beetle, the 1961 VW 1500 had its engine at the rear. The whitewall tyres are one of the most distinctive features of Tekno models.
Price guide: £90

Tekno 824 MGA

Tekno was by no means the only company to reproduce the MGA in diecast form but this version is unique in representing a hardtop coupé. The model shown has the same wheels as the TD, but also features more modern refinements, such as glazed windows, spring suspension, plastic headlamp lenses and – a particular Tekno trademark – a high quality transfer on the boot representing the MG logo and 1600 script.
Price guide: £125

Tekno 824 Ford Taunus 17M

Tekno's version of the 17M is more accurate than the German Gama. In addition to window glazing it features separate bumpers, headlamp lenses and a diecast base.
Price guide: £125

Tekno 826 Ford Taunus 17M

The rounded shape of the next generation of Ford Taunus, produced between 1960 and 1964, gave rise to the nickname 'badewanne' ('bathtub'). The Tekno has interior fittings and suspension.
Price guide: £100

Tekno 826 Ford Taunus 17M Police

The police version of the Taunus has a 'Stop' sign at the rear and a removable plastic roof light.
Price guide: £100

Tekno 924 Mercedes-Benz 300SL
This model had an opening boot and bonnet and came in either open or hardtop form. Note the box label which indicates that Tekno products were distributed in France by Solido.
Price guide: £90
(Courtesy David G Ralston)

Tekno 413 Volkswagen Van 'Philips'
More than fifty different liveries were produced on this casting, many of them in limited quantities. The 'Philips' van was more widely distributed and is pictured in some catalogues.
Price guide: £150

Tekno 413 Volkswagen Van 'Mobeltransport'
One of the harder to find vans is this one in the colours of a removals firm. A similar livery was also used on a larger articulated Volvo truck.
Price guide: £250

Tekno 405 Volkswagen van 'BP'
In 1959 a new and more detailed van casting was introduced which, like its predecessor, was made in two halves to facilitate two-tone finishes.
Price guide: £150

OTHER EUROPEAN COUNTRIES

Tekno 410 Volkswagen Pick-up 'Firestone'
A variation of the 405 van casting, this pick-up carries a spare tyre in the rear compartment.
Price guide: £150

Tekno 419 Ford Taunus van 'Empera'
As with the Volkswagen, multiple liveries can be found on the Ford Taunus casting. No other diecast manufacturer could match Tekno's skill in designing and fitting colourful transfers.
Price guide: £250

Tekno 415 Ford Taunus Van 'Dunlop'
The attractive logo used on this van is based on a contemporary advertisement for Dunlop tyres.
Price guide: £250

Tekno 415 Ford Taunus Van 'Jensen and Møller'
Tekno liveries typically cover the sides, rear and roof of the model. This one appears to advertise a brand of biscuits.
Price guide: £250

Tekno 850 Volvo Bus

A vast number of different liveries appeared on this Volvo bus, some with a slot in the roof so that the toy could be used as a savings bank. This extremely rare example is in the livery of Max J. Madsen, a Danish bus operator.
Price guide: £400
(Courtesy Bruce Sterling)

Vilmer 342 Cattle Truck

This four-inch Dodge truck closely resembles the one in the Tekno range.
Price guide: £75
(Courtesy Douglas R Kelly)

Vilmer 344 'Carlsberg' Truck

Vans with advertising tend to fetch a higher premium, as is the case with this one in the livery of the Danish brewer Carlsberg.
Price guide: £90
(Courtesy Douglas R Kelly)

Vilmer 346 Wrecking Car

Another variation on the Vilmer Dodge. The roof-mounted spare wheel steers the front axle and the grille is a separate tinplate component.
Price guide: £75
(Courtesy Douglas R Kelly)

OTHER EUROPEAN COUNTRIES

Metosul Volkswagen
This Portuguese model was based on the earlier Dinky Toy casting, with the
addition of suspension and a plastic interior but, unusually, no window glazing.
Price guide: £20

Metosul Volkswagen
A number of different liveries appeared on the Metosul Volkswagen, including 'Brigada
de Transito,' the traffic force of the Guarda Nacional Republicana.
Price guide: £20

Metosul Atlantean Bus
Another Metosul model with obvious Dinky ancestry. Note, however, that the entrance
doors are on the opposite side as the vehicle would have been left-hand drive. Many
different liveries can be found.
Price guide: £25

Lenyko Volvo PV444
A Gothenburg toy wholesaler produced this model between 1958 and 1963. Scale
is approximately 1/45 and the car can be found with either a one-piece or split
windscreen.
Price guide: £175

Lemeco Ford 'Polis' Car
Although it has many similarities to the Dinky Toy version, this model is not a reissue or exact copy. The fragile roof top accessories make it an extremely rare item.
Price guide: £275+
(Courtesy Alex J Cameron)

Lion Car DKW 3=6
The German DKW has been rarely modelled, making this Lion Car version highly desirable. Described as being to 1/45 scale, it was introduced in 1956 or 1957.
Price guide: £125

Lion Car Renault Dauphine
The Dauphine was the fifth car modelled by Lion Car. Later issues had window glazing and interior fittings.
Price guide: £120

Best Box 2313 Jaguar E Type and 2516 Mercedes 250 SE Coupé
Another Dutch series was Best Box, which made Matchbox-size cars. Both these models have suspension and opening doors.
Price guide: £20 each

OTHER EUROPEAN COUNTRIES

Gasquy Chevrolet
This very rare Gasquy model from Belgium represents a 1949 Chevrolet Styleline.
Price guide: £250
(Courtesy Douglas R Kelly)

Gasquy Tatra
The rear-engined Czechoslovakian T600 Tatraplan was in production between 1947 and 1952. This is the most desirable Gasquy model as it is one of the very few replicas of the car.
Price guide: £300+
(Courtesy Douglas R Kelly)

Gasquy Sep-Toy Stake Truck
This simple truck is based on a 1940s prototype by FN (Fabrique Nationale), a Belgian manufacturer of firearms, motorcycles and commercial vehicles.
Price guide: £50

Sablon 5 BMW 1600
Although the body castings of the Belgian Sablon range were well made, the plastic used on the wheels tends to distort, making perfect examples virtually impossible to find. On this example, the front wheels have been replaced.
Price guide: £25

USA

n the early years of the twentieth century America dominated the mass production of diecast toy cars as well as of the real thing. Strangely, after such an auspicious start, the United States never really became a world leader in the diecast field. For instance, over the next half century the products in the pioneering Tootsietoy series did not develop much further than the original concept of a simple bodyshell on wheels.

Admittedly, 'a simple bodyshell on wheels' could be a description of virtually any diecast toy made anywhere in the world up until the late 1950s, when – as earlier chapters have shown – companies like Corgi in Britain, Solido in France and Tekno in Denmark began to develop more and more refinements, such as window glazing, suspension and opening parts. American diecast makers, such as Tootsietoys, Midgetoys and Goodee Toys never attempted to compete with these and continued to produce simple, unsophisticated toy cars.

One reason for this might be that the United States was the major export market for many European companies and the presence on the American market of so many high quality imported diecasts may have led homegrown toy manufacturers to concentrate on other toy lines instead, such as Buddy 'L' and Tonka pressed steel toys, or the many 1/25 scale plastic promotional models made for General Motors, Ford and the other motor corporations. Even more significantly, by the late 1950s high-quality scale model cars in kit form by companies like Revell were becoming very popular.

Tootsietoys

Tootsietoys – the world's first diecast models was the title of a book published in 1980 by two American enthusiasts, James Wieland and Edward Force, who traced the history of the company in detail. Since then, other authors have retold the story so that information on dates, models and colour variations is not difficult to come by. Although recent research suggests that Tootsietoys may not, in fact, have made the 'world's first diecast models' – that honour may belong to a French firm, SR of Paris[1] – the American company can, nevertheless, claim to have popularised the concept.

Towards the end of the nineteenth century Charles O Dowst of Chicago began to make small castings, such as buttons and bracelet

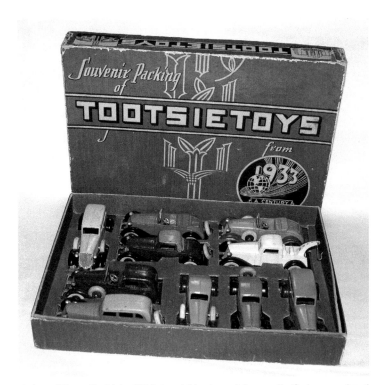

An incredibly rare Tootsietoy Gift Set containing ten variations on the Graham, produced for the 1933 Chicago World Fair.
(Courtesy Gary Cohen)

charms. The first toy car arrived in 1911, and a Model T Ford followed, probably in 1916. The Tootsietoy name was registered in 1924 and nine years later the company was making good quality models of an American car called the Graham Blue Streak, with streamlined styling that was advanced for its day. The models were equally advanced in their design: according to Wieland and Force, they introduced the three-part construction (radiator, body and chassis) which was soon afterwards copied in the UK by Meccano Limited. Of even greater

tootsietoys

NEW! displays, models and sets

NEW! packaging, extra play value

NEW! impact and appeal

tootsietoy Truck Terminal Set
7 X-act model die-cast metal trucks in hi-gloss baked enamel finishes. Includes Van Trailer—Auto Transport—Oil Tanker—Logger—Local Hauling Truck—Metro Delivery Truck and Tow Truck. Packed in rubber-like freight dock; Corrugated outer shipper makes up as freight terminal. Wt. 3¾ lbs.
37N123X380 .... Retail 6.00

tootsietoy Turnpike Set
8 realistic model die cast metal trucks and cars including Greyhound Scenicruiser — U-Haul Trailer — Oil Tanker — Van Trailer—sedan—sport coupe—station wagon and convertible. Durable baked-on hi-gloss finishes. Packed in rubber-like turnpike plaza. Attractive full-color box. Wt. 3 lbs.
37N119X317 .... Retail 5.00

tootsietoy Playtime Village Set
9 X-act model die-cast tootsietoys. Includes 2 airplanes, 1 tow truck, 1 panel truck, 1 station wagon, 1 convertible, 1 sport coupe, 1 sedan, 1 hot rod and 10 metal road signs. Hi-gloss baked enamel finish. Rubber-like tray makes into gas pumps, garage and hangar. Packed in 4-color box. Wt. 2¼ lbs.
37N122X254 .... Retail 4.00

tootsietoy Combat Set
15 pieces. Authentic scale models in die-cast metal. Includes atomic tank that moves on rubber caterpillar tread; turret revolves; gun raises and lowers. 155 mm cannon shoots harmless wood pellets; rolls on large rubber tires. 3 jet planes, convoy truck, ambulance, command car, jeep and 6 polyethylene soldiers. Realistic OD hi-gloss finish. Each in 4 color box. Wt. 2¾ lbs.
37N118X254 .... Retail 4.00

A 1959 Tootsietoys trade advertisement showing a selection from this extensive range. These cheap but colourful toys were often sold in sets as well as individually.

importance was the fact that Tootsietoys were now made from zinc alloy ('Zamak') rather than lead, allowing for more precise casting details. In 1935 the Tootsietoy firm surpassed itself with its La Salle models (a General Motors marque sometimes described as a 'junior-grade Cadillac').

Postwar, Tootsietoys never regained such heights of realism, concentrating instead on much simpler cars – so simple that in some cases the axles were threaded through from one side of the body to the other without the wheel arches being cut out. These cars were available in three-inch, four-inch and six-inch series. Some of the larger ones had individual boxes, but typical Tootsietoy packaging consisted of a simple 'bubble pack' design. These toys were also sold in gift sets together with roadside accessories.

Hubley

In 1893 John Edward Hubley founded a company in Lancaster, Pennsylvania to manufacture metal toys such as ferris wheels and trains. After his death in 1900 the company was taken over by John H Hartman and Joseph T Breneman whose families remained in control until 1966. Many large, heavy cast iron toy vehicles were made throughout the '20s and '30s but these gave way to diecasts from 1936 onwards, the earliest being a 3.5-inch long sedan with rubber wheels, not based on any particular real car. As with most other toy companies, production halted during the Second World War but took off in a bigger way in the fifties when many new lines were introduced, not only in diecast but, increasingly, in plastic.

One thing that differentiates Hubley cars from Tootsietoys is that they tend to be larger – anything from 6 to 12 inches long. Most are reasonable likenesses of real vehicles, mainly American, although two British sports cars, a Jaguar and an MG, were included in the range on account of the popularity of these in the USA at the time. Both were introduced in 1954; the Jaguar is 7.5in long and the MG 9in, being joined the following year by a smaller 6in version. Hubley's commercial vehicles were larger still, with some articulated trucks being as much as 18 inches long. Ford enthusiasts are particularly well catered for, and there are many tow trucks, stake trucks, log carriers and dumpers. Hubley's most unusual model must surely be the 1958 Ford in 'US Fish Hatchery' livery which came with a transparent plastic rear section that could be filled with water with eight plastic fish swimming in it. There was even a fishing net supplied to catch them!

In 1960 Hubley changed direction and introduced a new range of smaller diecasts in 1/60 scale called 'Real Toys.' The slightly unusual scale of these places them half-way between Dinky and Matchbox-size – rather like the later British Lone Star Impy series or the German Sikus. Curiously, the smaller they grew, the more realistic the Hubley models became and the Real Toys provide an interesting lineup of popular American cars like the Ford Fairlane, Chrysler Imperial and Ford Falcon. These were supplied with 'customising decals' with which the child could personalise his toy.

Every model car range contains interesting variations but in the case of Hubley the collector can try to find not simply one or two different colour schemes but the entire range twice over. The reason is that the models were sold in the USA as Real Toys, whereas in Canada they bore the name of Real Types. Body castings appear to be the same but the baseplate lettering is different and there are some local variants, too, such as the Metro delivery van in the livery of a department store, Eaton's of Canada.

Produced between 1960 and 1964, Real Toys were the

The first issue was the 'four-in-one' truck set of 1946, comprising a cab unit and three alternative body sections. In 1948 came the most recognisable Midgetoy, the 'futuristic auto' which was so popular that it remained in production until the late 1960s. Most Midgetoys averaged 3.5 inches in length, but there were also the smaller 'Midgets,' larger 'King Size' models, and six-inch 'Jumbos.'

Production continued into the 1970s but surplus stocks were still available in the 1980s when some models were sold on the collectors' market accompanied by a 'certificate of authenticity' signed by the Herdklotz brothers.[2]

Goodee Toys

Like Midgetoys, Goodee is another brand that made toy cars in a very similar style to Tootsietoys. The manufacturer was Excel Products of East Brunswick, New Jersey, and the most interesting subjects are a Lincoln Capri coupé, a Studebaker, and a surprisingly realistic Cadillac Eldorado convertible, all based on 1953 prototypes. In addition to the cars, there were a number of diecast trucks and aeroplanes.

Like Tootsietoys, some of these came in two sizes (3 or 6 inches) and they were made in exactly the same style, with filled-in wheelarches to allow the rubber wheels to be fitted simply by inserting an axle through both sides of the body. Wheels seem to have been fitted prior to painting and masking was often rudimentary, so that paint gets onto the tyres.

Production is not thought to have continued beyond 1958, which suggests that Goodee Toys didn't make much of an impact on the toy market as there was little to distinguish the models from those of the brand-leading Tootsietoys.

Slik-Toy

The Lansing Company Inc. was the largest factory in the small town of Lansing, Iowa, on the banks of the Mississippi. Founded to manufacture buttons in 1897, the company gained casting and moulding skills and later diversified into other product lines, such as toys. In the 1940s Lansing made a number of seven-inch vehicles from aluminium rather than the usual zinc alloy. These were sold under the name Slik-Toys and the catalogue was not slow to point out the advantages of aluminium to the trader: the toys were 'stronger' and 'lighter' and as such 'the shipping weights are considerably lower than a similar toy made of heavier metal.' The range consisted of a fastback coupé car, an open pick-up, stake truck and tanker. There were also tractors, farm implements, construction plant models, and some 4.5-inch plastic cars and trucks. Toy manufacture ceased around 1956 – though the company is still making buttons!

Ertl

Another Iowa firm that exploited the farm toy market on a much bigger scale was Ertl. Fred Ertl was of German origin and at the end of World War Two held down a modest job as a journeyman moulder. Finding himself unemployed, but with six children to feed, he was forced to look for an alternative income and adapted his metal-working skills to the production of toy tractors, made in the basement of his house from melted down war-surplus aluminium. His sons then toured Iowa and

Cover of a mid-1950s catalogue showing the 1/48 scale trucks made by the Ralston Toy and Novelty Company of Nebraska.

most realistic diecasts Hubley ever made. As with many other manufacturers, though, things went steadily downhill thereafter. The company was purchased by Gabriel Industries in 1966; a decade later, the Hubley name had disappeared.

Midgetoys

Midgetoy is a more obscure brand than Tootsietoys or Hubley, but thanks to the researches of American collector and toy historian Douglas R Kelly, a good deal is known about this company. Brothers Alvin and Earl Herdklotz ran the A & E Tool and Gage Company in Rockford, Illinois, making dies for other companies during the Second World War. Postwar, the brothers diversified into toys that were made as simply as possible in order to undercut the competition.

sold the toys to retailers in the many small farming towns in the area where they found a ready market.

Ertl's big break came when he secured a contract with the John Deere company whose tractor plant was in his home town of Dubuque. Ertl was now in effect manufacturing promotional models, rather like the 1/25 scale model cars that American car manufacturers used as showroom giveaways at the time. Similar deals were soon signed with other farm equipment companies like Case, Ford, Deutz, and Massey Ferguson. Before long, production had moved to a 16,000 square foot factory in Dyersville.

Fifty years on, Ertl is still the big name in farm toys and Dyersville promotes itself as the 'Farm Toy Capital of the World' and houses a National Farm Toy museum. In addition to the ever-expanding range of farm toys, Ertl has gone on to make many other diecast product lines including classic cars, cartoon-related character merchandise, and 'custom imprint' banks, which are limited edition diecast vans with a slot in the roof for saving coins – though it's most unlikely that any collector uses them for this purpose!

Other brands
Manoil, like Midgetoy, was founded by two brothers. Jack and Maurice Manoil made metal toys in various factories in the vicinity of New York between 1927 and 1955. The first Manoil cars appeared in 1934, but most tended to be based on futuristic 'art deco' styling rather than on real prototypes.

Two other American brands are associated with model trucks rather than cars. Before World War Two, Ralstoy (short for Ralston Toy and Novelty Company of Ralston, Nebraska) made metal toy vehicles before turning to wood as a result of wartime shortages of raw materials. After the war Ralstoy started to make diecast articulated trucks, and production continues today with simple vans that businesses can order with their own lettering and logos for promotional purposes. Another company which offers a similar service on a larger scale is Winross of Churchville, NY. The original Winross company had started to make model trucks in the early 1960s, many of them based on White prototypes.

Hot Wheels
In 1968, everything changed on the American diecast market – and indeed, throughout the world. Elliot Handler, co-founder of Mattel Toys, was enjoying huge success with the Barbie doll for girls and was looking to expand his product line. He asked research and development specialist Jack Ryan to design a new range of diecast cars. Ryan involved General Motors' designer Harry Bradley in the project, and the story goes that it was Handler's comment on Bradley's own custom hot rod car – "Man, those are some hot wheels!" – that gave the new range its name.

REAL-TOYS
ALL METAL BODY
RUBBER TIRES
PLASTIC WINDOWS

ALL REAL-TOYS INDIVIDUALLY CARDED OR IN COLLECTORS' DISPLAY TUBE.

by ▶Hubley®

SUGGESTED RETAIL – $.79		WEIGHT PER CARTON
420 420R	CHEVROLET CORVETTE	6 LBS.
421 421R	FORD THUNDERBIRD	6 LBS.
422 422R	STUDEBAKER HAWK	6 LBS.
423 423R	CHRYSLER IMPERIAL	6 LBS.

SUGGESTED RETAIL – $.79		WEIGHT PER CARTON
424 424R	CHEVROLET PICKUP	6 LBS.
425 425R	FORD FALCON	6 LBS.
426 426R	CHEVROLET CORVAIR	6 LBS.
427 427R	FORD COUNTRY SQUIRE	6 LBS.

SUGGESTED RETAIL – $.79		WEIGHT PER CARTON
428 428R	BUICK	6 LBS.
550 550R	GM FIREBIRD III	6 LBS.
551 551R	FORD PANEL TRUCK	6 LBS.
552 552R	CHEVROLET AMBULANCE	6 LBS.

1/60TH SCALE MODELS OF POPULAR AMERICAN VEHICLES

EACH CAR COMPLETE WITH CUSTOMIZING DECALS AND EXCITING CLUB OFFER FOR COLLECTORS

c.1960 trade advertisement for Hubley's Real-Toys, described as 'a series of 1/60 scale models of popular American vehicles.'

Instead of the crude style of toy made by Tootsietoy, Midgetoy or Goodee, Mattel at last offered American youngsters something much more stylish and modern: customised Mustangs and Firebirds with torsion bar suspension, vinyl roofs 'spectraflame paint,' and fast-running low-friction wheels that allowed the cars to race up and down specially-designed plastic tracks and perform somersaults. Even the tone of language used in the catalogue must have made these cars sound so much more exciting to children at the time: "Hot Wheels

Cover of the UK edition of the 1967 catalogue of Hot Wheels, the 'fastest metal cars in the world.'

are the fastest metal cars in the world! They don't need batteries, or electrical current or motors – yet they out-race, out-stunt, out-distance every other miniature metal car ... Collect 'em! Race 'em! Show 'em off!"

There were initially sixteen cars when the range was launched in 1968 and they were an instant hit. Sales of imported competitors – Matchbox, Impy, Siku – plummeted, and these makers were forced to redesign their products in an attempt to keep up. Sales of larger diecasts like Dinky and Corgi suffered, too, and these soon began to feature 'speedwheels' and 'whizzwheels,' though their size and weight made them unsuitable to run on tracks like Hot Wheels. For many collectors of 'traditional' diecast cars, this marked the end of an era: these wheels may have increased play value but they detracted from the realism of the models.

Hot Wheels continue to have a huge following today and, of course, the earliest products are now valuable collectors' items in their own right, especially if sealed in the original packaging. By the time of Hot Wheels' fortieth anniversary in 2008 an estimated four billion cars had been made – an event which Mattel celebrated by producing a special edition model in 18-carat gold, decorated with over 27,000 diamonds and valued at £72,000!

Custom Cougars and Mustangs were very different from the kind of cars offered by most other manufacturers, whose sales suffered as result of Hot Wheels' success.

 # 6205 Custom COUGAR
Mercury hardtop with California Styling: Side Pipes. Twin Power Bulges. Working Hood. Raked Body. Red Stripe Tyres. 'Mag' Wheels. Detailed Underbody. Customized Engine. Orange or blue.

 # 6206 Custom MUSTANG
Ford fastback with California Styling: Side Pipes. Power Bulge. Working Hood. Raked Body. Red Stripe Tyres. 'Mag' Wheels. Detailed Underbody. Customized Engine. Red or gold.

 # 6207 Custom T-BIRD
Ford hardtop with California Styling: Side Pipes. Power Bulge. Working Hood. Raked Body. Red Stripe Tyres. 'Mag' Wheels. Detailed Underbody. Customized Engine. Black "Vinyl" Roof. Aqua or gold.

 # 6208 Custom CAMARO
Chevrolet hardtop with California Styling: Side Pipes. Twin Power Bulges. Working Hood. Raked Body. Red Stripe Tyres . 'Mag' Wheels. Detailed Underbody. Customized Engine. Black "Vinyl" roof. Lime or blue.

[1] See www.tootsietoys.info
[2] See The Die Cast Price Guide by Douglas R Kelly for full details of the Midgetoy story.

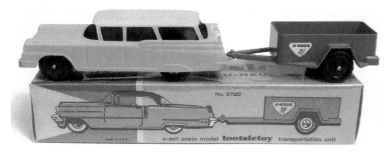

Tootsietoys 3720 U-Haul set

Although the box depicts a Cadillac, the car inside is a 1959 Ford Station Wagon, one of a series of six-inch 1950s cars from Tootsietoys which included a Packard Patrician, Lincoln Capri, and Chrysler New Yorker. The Ford comes hitched to an orange trailer with a U-Haul sticker. The idea was that a trailer could be hired for a one-way journey and deposited at a U-Haul dealership in another town.
Price guide: £100

Tootsietoys 869 Utility Truck

An impressive 9-inch long articulated truck based on a 1947 Mack. The trailer has five removable stake sections.
Price guide: £100

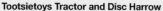

Tootsietoys Greyhound Bus

A six-inch model of the 1957 Greyhound Scenicruiser bus. The casting is made in two halves and is the third Greyhound bus to be modelled by Tootsietoys.
Price guide: £75

Tootsietoys Tractor and Disc Harrow

Although not identified as such, the Tootsietoy tractor resembles the 1939-52 Ford N Type. The model was introduced in 1952 and was still available in 1969. A strong and robust toy with one-piece rubber wheels, the tractor can also be found fitted with a movable scoop at the front and towing a trailer.
Price guide: £80

Tootsietoys Fords
Many Tootsietoy cars were made in both three- and four-inch sizes. These are examples of the smaller series and represent a 1955 Ford Thunderbird and a 1955 Ford Customline.
Price guide: £10 each

Tootsietoys Ford and Oldsmobile
Four-inch 1954 Ford Ranch Wagon and 1955 Oldsmobile 98 Holiday. The price sticker on the roof is original.
Price guide: £10 each

Tootsietoys 7250 'Motors' Gift Set
This scarce1950s set contains four six-inch models: a Shell tanker, Greyhound coach, Chrysler Windsor, and Cadillac.
Price guide: £400
(Courtesy Gary Cohen)

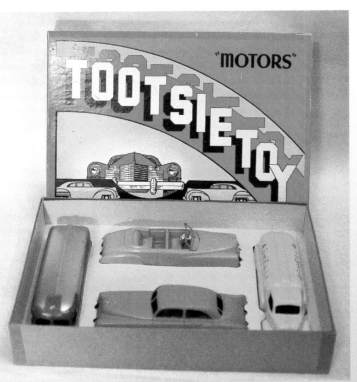

Hubley 486 Deluxe Sports Car
This heavy, nine-inch long convertible, introduced in 1956, is a reasonably accurate likeness of the Ford Thunderbird. The removable roof is moulded in plastic.
Price guide: £100

Hubley 454 Log Truck
First shown in the 1954 Hubley catalogue, this Ford log truck is 7.5 inches long and comes with five wooden logs.
Price guide: £75

Hubley Real Toys 554 Ford Taxi
The 1/60 scale Real Toys series was supplied in transparent plastic cases and came with transfers (known as 'decals' in the USA) which the owner could apply.
Price guide: £75
(Courtesy Douglas R Kelly)

Hubley Real Toys 426 Chevrolet Corvair
The 'customizing decals' supplied with this model read 'Tom's Tobacco Shop,' which would hardly be deemed suitable on a toy today!
Price guide: £60
(Courtesy Douglas R Kelly)

Hubley Real Toys 425 Ford Falcon
The Falcon, like the Corvair, was one of the smaller 'compact' sized American cars of the early 1960s.
Price guide: £60
(Courtesy Douglas R Kelly)

Hubley Real Toys 423 Chrysler Imperial
This example is a rare survivor which has remained sealed in its plastic case for nearly half a century!
Price guide: £65
(Courtesy Douglas R Kelly)

Renwal 147 Convertible
This model, like other diecasts by Renwal, dates from 1955 and was also made in plastic.
Price guide: £30
(Courtesy Douglas R Kelly)

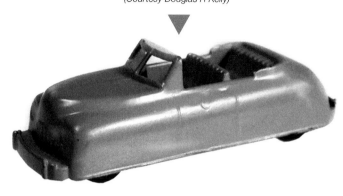

Irwin Buick
Founded in 1922, Irwin made many plastic toys, but this scarce four-inch Buick is a diecast product. It is powered by a friction mechanism.
Price guide: £50
(Courtesy Douglas R Kelly)

Midgetoys
The Futuristic Car (centre) was one of the most popular Midgetoys, remaining in production from 1948 until the 1960s. The bus and 'Hot Rod' car are typical American vehicles of the period.
Price guide: £8 each

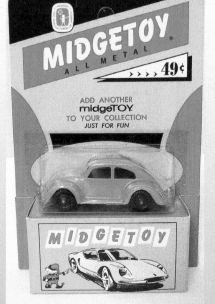

Midgetoy Volkswagen
Nearly 200,000 Volkswagen Beetles were sold in the USA in 1960, making it a good year for Midgetoy to bring out this 2.5-inch model.
Price guide: £10

Midgetoy Pick-up
Part of the six-inch 'Jumbo' series, this pick-up truck is unusual in having a printed cardboard section in the rear compartment.
Price guide: £10

USA

Midgetoy Truck set
Dating from 1946, the '4 in 1' Truck set was the first item in the Midgetoy series. The three alternative bodies can be fitted onto the 3-inch truck chassis.
Price guide: £25

Winross Firestone Truck
The cab of this truck is based on a White 3000, the first casting made by Winross in 1963. Scale is said to be 1/64.
Price Guide: £50

Slik-Toy Car
Dating from around 1946, this aluminium model represents a generic forties-style American car of the 'fastback' coupé type. 7 inches in length, it has an open base and solid rubber tyres, and can also be found as a taxi.
Price guide: £40

Goodee set
A scarce gift set containing six vehicles and a cardboard service station kit. Any attempt to assemble the building would, of course, destroy the original packaging.
Price guide: £100+

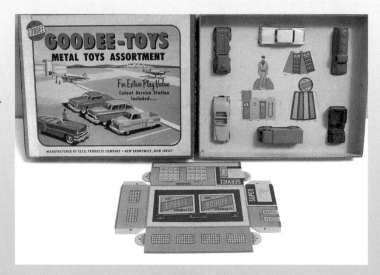

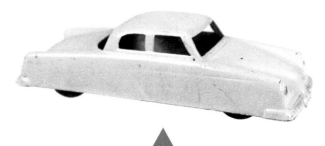

Goodee Lincolns

Two colour variations on the three-inch diecast model of the 1953 Lincoln Capri by Goodee. The overspray on the wheels is original: clearly, the toys were assembled first and quickly spray-painted afterwards.
Price guide: £8

Goodee Studebaker

Based on the 1953 Studebaker Champion, this Goodee toy has covered wheelarches. The style of the model is similar to contemporary Tootsietoys.
Price guide: £8
(Courtesy Douglas R Kelly)

Barclay Sedan

This 3.25-inch sedan by Barclay of New Jersey dates from the 1930s and is typical of the lead alloy toys of the period.
Price guide: £35
(Courtesy Douglas R Kelly)

Barclay Euclid Truck

Barclay's 'Metal Mites' was a range of two-inch diecast vehicles, mostly trucks, which came in a bubble-pack shaped like a miniature bottle.
Price guide: £10

Beaut Sedan

This crudely-made 3.75-inch sedan from the Beaut Manufacturing Company of New Jersey dates from the period 1946-50.
Price guide: £10
(Courtesy Douglas R Kelly)

Londontoys Chevrolet Master Deluxe Coupé

Based on a 1940s Chevrolet, this model was made in London, Ontario, Canada, but was also produced in the USA. Like some others in the range, both four- and six-inch versions exist.
Price guide: £15
(Courtesy Douglas R Kelly)

USA

Ralstoy Removals Truck
One of the most attractive liveries to be found on the Ralstoy Ford box van. Total model length is 8.5 inches.
Price guide: £60

Ralstoy Oldsmobile
This six-inch, chrome-plated toy is not typical of Ralstoy products, most of which were trucks. The car is based on a 1948 Oldsmobile.
Price guide: £15

Hot Wheels 6404 Classic Nomad
Hot Wheels cars were radically different from earlier diecast toys. Early issues had 'redline' wheels, as on this item, which was produced in 1970-71.
Price guide: £90
(Courtesy Douglas R Kelly)

Hot Wheels 6421 Jack Rabbit Special
Until 1972, Hot Wheels cars came with a tinplate 'collector's button.' Models in unopened packaging are worth significantly more than loose items.
Price Guide: £35
(Courtesy Douglas R Kelly)

JAPAN

During the 1950s most Japanese toy cars were made of tinplate rather than diecast metal, and were powered by friction or electric motors. Tinplate toys had been made in Japan before the Second World War, but they reached new heights of realism in the fifties. The postwar American occupation of Japan gave Japanese toymakers access to the lucrative American market, and for this reason most of the tinplate toy cars made in the period were based on American vehicles: Cadillacs, Chevrolets, Oldsmobiles, Buicks, Fords, and many others.

These were big toys, with some being sixteen inches in length, compared with four inches for the average diecast model. As such, tinplate was the ideal medium to capture the extravagant style of the American cars of the period, where size mattered and manufacturers vied with each other to fit increasingly powerful V8 engines, higher tail fins, and more and more chrome.

However, fashions change and tin toys fell out of favour in the 1960s, partly because of safety concerns about sharp edges and partly because similar friction-powered toy cars could be produced more cheaply in plastic in Hong Kong. Always good at spotting the potential of a new market, Japanese toy companies accordingly turned their attention to making smaller-scale diecast cars.

The earliest recognisable Japanese diecast brand is the Silver Pet range made by Masudaya, one of the oldest Japanese toy companies. Just four cars are known: a Buick, a Ford Thunderbird, a Continental and a Cadillac Eldorado, all of them from the 1954-56 period. The name Silver Pet was chosen because the cars had a chrome-plated finish and the choice of exclusively American subjects suggests that they were originally intended for export to the USA where many of Masudaya's tin toys were already sold under the trademark MT (Modern Toys).

Next came the Collectoy series, made by Kuramochi Shoten for distribution by the Louis Marx company under their Linemar trademark. These are around 1/55 scale and comprise six American vehicles of c. 1958 vintage: Ford delivery van, Edsel, Buick, Lincoln Premiere, Chevrolet and Pontiac. Later these were joined by a batch of six European sports cars: Jaguar XK 150, Triumph TR3, BMW 507, Porsche 356, Mercedes 300SL and Chevrolet Corvette.

Another tin toy maker, Marusan, made a group of seven diecast cars around 1960, all of them either copied from Dinky Toys or made from second-hand tooling bought from the Meccano Company. Five were English (Austin van, Morris mail van, Daimler ambulance, Observation Coach and Euclid dump truck) and two French (a Ford milk truck and a Panhard articulated lorry). The only original casting was a Toyota pick-up truck.

Apart from the Toyota, very few of these models would ever have been seen on Japanese roads in real life. The first major 1/43 range designed specifically for the Japanese market came from the Asahi Toy Company in 1959. This new range, called Model Pet, consisted of vehicles to be seen on the roads of Tokyo and other Japanese cities, built by indigenous motor manufacturers such as Toyota, Nissan, Isuzu, Hino and Prince. The choice of a British Hillman Minx and Austin A50 Cambridge may seem anomalous but these were included in the range, as the real cars were assembled in Japan as a result of licensing agreements between the Rootes group and Isuzu and between Austin and Nissan. As well as making diecast and tinplate toys, the Asahi Company also acted as the Japanese distributor for Dinky and Corgi Toys, and the style of Model Pets was clearly influenced by early Corgi products, as can be seen from the similar wheels and the fitting of window glazing.

But toymaking is a competitive business, and Model Pet did not have the market to itself for long, as another range, Micro Pet, was launched in 1961 by the Taiseiya Company. The similarity between the names may have made it difficult for the newcomer to establish itself, and Micro Pets were quickly rebranded as Cherryca Phenix – a range which is now as legendary as the mythical creature after which it was named, albeit in a misspelt form!

To Japanese diecast specialists, Cherryca Phenix always represented the 'holy grail'; partly because the short production span makes them very rare, but also because of the unusual way they're made (from a softer and shinier type of metal called antimony). Most diecasts have details like lights and grilles painted on afterwards, but Cherryca did things the other way round: masking during the painting process allowed the bare metal to show through on bumpers, grilles and window frames, giving a 'chrome' effect.

走る！ミニチュアモデルカー

NO.10 シボレー・ハイ ウエイパトロール (Chevrolet Highway Patrol) 縮尺率 (Scale) $\frac{1}{52}$ 塗色 ¥250	NO.12 フォード・ファルコン (Ford Falcon) 縮尺率 (Scale) $\frac{1}{52}$ 塗色 ¥240・金色 ¥240	NO.9 シボレー・インパラ (Chevrolet Impala) 縮尺率 (Scale) $\frac{1}{52}$ 塗色 ¥250・金色 ¥250	NO.7 マツダ・R 360・クーペ (Mazda R360 クーペ) 縮尺率 (Scale) $\frac{1}{35}$ 塗色 ¥170・金色 ¥190
メルセデス・ベンツ 300SL (Mercedes Benz 300SL) 縮尺率 (Scale) $\frac{1}{50}$ 6月発売をめざして目下製作中	NO.8 トヨペット・ コロナライン (Toyopet Corona Line) 縮尺率 (Scale) $\frac{1}{45}$ 塗色 ¥180・金色 ¥200	NO.14 プリンス・ マイクロバス (Prince Micro-bus) 縮尺率 (Scale) $\frac{1}{47}$ 塗色 ¥210・金色 ¥220	NO.17 ダットサン・ ライトバン (Datsun Light Van) 縮尺率 (Scale) $\frac{1}{47}$ 塗色 ¥180・金色 ¥200

As this page from the 1961 catalogue shows, Micro Pet also made American cars such as the Ford Falcon (no. 12) and the Chevrolet Impala (nos. 9 and 10). (Courtesy Bruce Sterling)

Another reason for the desirability of this series lies in the variety of subjects chosen, combining a good selection of contemporary European, American and Japanese vehicles, including a Citroën DS 19 convertible, Volkswagen Beetle, Volkswagen Karmann Ghia Convertible, Ford Falcon, Buick Electra, Dodge Polara, and Cadillac 62.

The Cherryca range only lasted until 1965, when the moulds were taken over by another large Japanese toy company, Yonezawa, who then launched a new series: Diapet. Quite a number of early Diapets were made from ex-Cherryca moulds, often with alterations to allow for opening doors, bonnets and boots to be fitted. Diapet also began to fit diecast baseplates instead of tinplate ones.

These early Diapet products – made between 1965 and 1967 – are highly-prized by specialist collectors and are now every bit as valuable as their Cherryca Phenix predecessors. They are packaged

in all-card boxes with a picture of the car on the lid, as opposed to the later 'window' boxes. In due course, Diapet moved beyond reworking ex-Cherryca models and developed its own lines, though the later models are not nearly as distinctive. Diapet continues in production today, now under the ownership of a large Japanese toy distributor, the Agatsuma Group.

However, the biggest name in current Japanese diecast is Tomica, which dates back to 1970 when a series of three-inch long diecast models of Japanese vehicles was launched by the Tomy Company. These were followed two years later by the Tomica Dandy line of 1/43 scale models, again based on Japanese subjects until 1977, when the first European vehicles appeared. Among the most desirable of the Dandy series are the Volkswagen and Citroën H delivery vans, both of which can be found in a large number of different liveries.

With nearly forty years of continuous production, Tomica's

inventory is now so extensive that many Japanese collectors specialise in this brand alone. In 2004, Tomica capitalised on collectors' interest in historic vehicles with the 'Limited Vintage' line of highly-detailed replicas of classic Japanese cars of the fifties and sixties. Thus, the development of Japanese diecast has come full circle, and many of the vehicles in the original Model Pet and Cherryca Phenix ranges are once again available in model form.

All items pictured in this chapter come from the collection of Bruce Sterling (New York), one of the world's most comprehensive collections of Japanese toy cars.

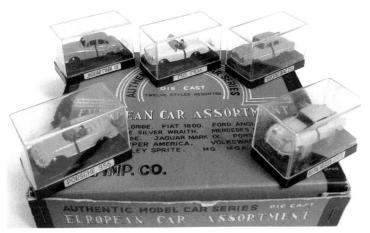

A set of one dozen 1.75-inch diecast models of European cars, marked 'Ace Imp. Co.,' which was clearly the importer or distributor rather than the manufacturer. Pictured here are: Porsche 356, Jaguar Mark IX, MGA, Mercedes-Benz 220, and Austin-Healey Sprite.

As well as manufacturing diecast cars, Japan played a key role in the development of the adult collecting hobby. As early as 1961 a Japanese Miniature Automobile Club (JMAC) existed and received encouragement from toy companies. The catalogue of the Taiseiya Micro Pet series not only illustrates the models available, but also includes advice on collecting and details of events for collectors. According to this document, "the Cafe Royal near the Toritsu Daigaku station in Tokyo is famous for its collection of miniature cars displayed in showcases. The cafe is a meeting place for collectors of miniature cars." There are even some brief biographies of Japanese toy collectors such as Mr Yasuyuki Ishida who lived in Tokyo and possessed a collection of 900 miniature cars. One day, we are told, the unfortunate Mr Ishida "left on a table a miniature of a rare European car, which he had managed to acquire at last. His cousin found it interesting and wanted to have it and Yasuyuki's mother gave it to him as a gift, not knowing its value to her son. Yasuyuki could not sleep that night." Similarly, the catalogue informs us that Mr Takaya Asada of Kanegawa-ken (pictured) "enjoys coming home after work and listening to Hawaiian music on his hi-fi set, whilst surrounded by his miniature cars."

Micro Pet 14 Prince Microbus
After the Second World War the company that made the famous Japanese Zero fighter planes diversified and became the Prince Motor Company. The name is said to be a tribute to Crown Prince Hirohito. This model of a Prince Microbus was made by the Taiseiya Company in 1961-62 as part of the short-lived Micro Pet series.
Price guide: £400
(Courtesy Bruce Sterling)

Cherryca Phenix PHE1 Hino Contessa
In 1962 the Micro Pet range was replaced by Cherryca Phenix, the first in the series being this 1961 Hino Contessa whose rear-engined layout was derived from the Renault 4CV which Hino had assembled for the Japanese market. This deep pink colour is particularly rare.
Price guide: £350+
(Courtesy Bruce Sterling)

Cherryca Phenix PHE 14 Isuzu Bellel
Isuzu originally assembled the Hillman Minx under licence but brought out its own car, the Bellel, in 1961. The Cherryca Phenix model is shown here in three different colour schemes.
Price guide: £200+
(Courtesy Bruce Sterling)

Cherryca Phenix PHE 34 Hino Contessa Sprint
Between 1962 and 1964 Hino offered this elegant one-litre coupé version of the Contessa. Note the opening rear engine compartment.
Price guide: £250+
(Courtesy Bruce Sterling)

Cherryca Phenix PHE 39 Prince Sprint

This unusual-looking coupé is based on a 1963 concept car which did not go into production. Other colour variations include metallic crimson and various shades of blue and green, in addition to the rare light yellow pictured here.
Price guide: £300+
(Courtesy Bruce Sterling)

Cherryca Phenix PHE 41 Daihatsu Berlina

Daihatsu produced this small car between1964 and 1967 and the Cherryca version can be found in either blue or off-white. Confusingly, the boxes of some Cherryca Phenix models continued to carry the earlier Micro Pet name.
Price guide: £150+
(Courtesy Bruce Sterling)

Cherryca Phenix Racing Saloons

In 1962 Honda built a test circuit at Suzuka, and the following year the first Grand Prix race was held there under the auspices of the Japan Automobile Federation (JAF). To coincide with the growing popularity of motor sport in Japan, Cherryca Phenix issued four of its cars in racing guise. According to one authority on Japanese toys, these represent vehicles that competed in the second Grand Prix in 1964. These models are essentially the same as the standard issues with the addition of racing transfers and boxes carrying photographs of the real vehicles. As such, they enabled Cherryca to offer something that looked new without incurring significant development costs. The four cars are (left-to-right): PHE 45 Mitsubishi Colt, PHE 46 Datsun Bluebird, PHE 47 Prince Skyline, and PHE 48 Prince Gloria. All are very rare as they were issued in small numbers towards the end of Cherryca Phenix production. A leaflet was supplied inside each box giving details of race results and speeds achieved.
Price guide: £400+ each
(Courtesy Bruce Sterling)

JAPAN

Cherryca Phenix PHE 45 Mitsubishi Colt
A close-up of the Mitsubishi Colt, showing the box illustration which depicts the real vehicle in action.
Price guide; £400+
(Courtesy Bruce Sterling)

Cherryca Phenix PHE 8 Volkswagen
Described as an 'Export Volkswagen,' this model of the Beetle can be found in green, dark blue or red. An interesting feature is that the plastic steering wheel is moulded in the same colour as the bodywork.
Price guide: £250+
(Courtesy Bruce Sterling)

Cherryca Phenix PHE9 Volkswagen Karmann Ghia
One of the most desirable of Cherryca's European cars, the Karmann Ghia is fitted with a plastic glazing unit that includes the side windows. The model on the left is in the later box style, with a wrapper indicating that it was supplied to a German toy distributor called Max Zapf.
Price guide: £400+
(Courtesy Bruce Sterling)

Cherryca Phenix PHE 18 Mercedes-Benz 220SE
Mercedes introduced the new generation of 'fintail' styling at the 1959 Frankfurt Motor Show, and by the time production of the series ended in 1968, some 973,000 cars had been built and exported all over the world. The Cherryca Phenix comes in black, red, yellow, cream, and this unusual metallic grey shade, which complements the grey tyres very well.
Price guide: £250+
(Courtesy Bruce Sterling)

Cherryca Phenix PHE 7 Ford Falcon

Originally issued as a Micro Pet no. F 12 and thereafter as a Cherryca Phenix, this model of Ford's 'compact' car, the 1960 Ford Falcon, can be found in many guises. The early Micro Pet version comes with or without battery-operated lights (the latter number 2 in the 'Flasher Lamp' series), and as a black and white police car. Some of the numerous attractive two-tone colour variations available are shown here.
Price guide: £250+
(Courtesy Bruce Sterling)

Cherryca Phenix PHE 10 Dodge Polara

The 1961 Dodge is one of the six American vehicles in the Cherryca Phenix series, and is shown here in three different colour schemes.
Price guide: £200+
(Courtesy Bruce Sterling)

Cherryca Phenix PHE 17 Lincoln Continental

Four colour variations on the Lincoln, the most common of the American car series. Tyres can be either grey or black.
Price guide: £175+
(Courtesy Bruce Sterling)

Cherryca Phenix PHE 20 Cadillac

The last American car to be issued was this 1962 Cadillac Special, shown here in metallic light blue, black and, rarest of all, yellow.
Price guide: £300+
(Courtesy Bruce Sterling)

JAPAN

Model Pet 2SA Toyota Masterline Ambulance
An ambulance based on the Toyopet Crown saloon. Model Pet also issued this item as a station wagon.
Price guide: £200
(Courtesy Bruce Sterling)

Model Pet 8 Austin A50 Cambridge
As the Austin A50 was assembled in Japan by Nissan under licence, it was a natural subject for Model Pet to choose. It looks best in two-tone red and white, but this dark blue version is the rarest.
Price guide: £300
(Courtesy Bruce Sterling)

Model Pet 9 Hillman Minx
An agreement with the Rootes Group allowed the Hillman Minx to be built in the Isuzu factory. Some versions of the Model Pet have spring suspension.
Price guide: £125
(Courtesy Bruce Sterling)

Model Pet 14 Toyota Publica
Launched in 1961, the Toyota Publica was designed as a small car to bring motoring to the masses, the thinking behind the name 'Publica' being not unlike Ford's Popular which similarly offered motoring at a budget price.
Price guide: £125
(Courtesy Bruce Sterling)

Model Pet 16 Prince Skyline Coupé

Designed by the Italian Michelotti, the Skyline went on sale in 1961, but only about 500 examples were built. A convertible was available and Model Pet also modelled this version.
Price guide: £125
(Courtesy Bruce Sterling)

Model Pet 18 Isuzu Bellel

A comparison of the Model Pet with the more elaborate Cherryca Phenix PHE 14 highlights the differences in style between the two manufacturers.
Price guide: £150
(Courtesy Bruce Sterling)

Model Pet 22 Prince Gloria Taxi

The Prince Gloria was a large and luxurious car which first appeared in 1961. This taxi is based on the 1966 model and has an opening bonnet and boot, and a triangular roof sign.
Price guide: £300
(Courtesy Bruce Sterling)

Model Pet 29 Hino Contessa Coupé

Another Italian design from Michelotti. The Model Pet version has opening front and rear compartments.
Price guide: £175
(Courtesy Bruce Sterling)

Model Pet 31 Toyota Sports 800
Available between 1965 and 1969, the 800 was Toyota's first production sports car. The Model Pet has an opening boot and bonnet and, as on the real car, the black roof section is removable.
Price guide: £175
(Courtesy Bruce Sterling)

Model Pet 34/35 Honda S800
The 1966 S800 was a more powerful version of the original S600. Model Pet offered the car in both convertible and coupé forms.
Price guide: £200
(Courtesy Bruce Sterling)

Model Pet 503 Road Sign set
There were relatively few accessory items made to accompany early Japanese diecasts, but Model Pet offered two different sets of road signs, each box (ref 502 and 503) containing sixteen metal signs.
Price guide: £150
(Courtesy Bruce Sterling)

Model Pet 504 Esso Petrol Pumps
The red and blue petrol pumps are moulded in plastic whereas the base is diecast metal.
Price guide: £150
(Courtesy Bruce Sterling)

Diapet D123 Mercedes-Benz 300SL Convertible

No fewer than four different Japanese variations of the Mercedes convertible have been identified. The earliest (left) was Cherryca Phenix PHE3, an open roadster in white with red seats. Cherryca Phenix PHE11 was the same model, with the addition of a removable hardtop roof section in red, made entirely of metal with a solid rear window. Later, Cherryca Phenix made a new casting (PHE29) with opening boot, bonnet and doors, and a rather heavy-looking chrome-plated section at the front which combines bumper, grille and lights. Colours are cream or red. This model found its way into the Diapet series as D123 (right). The front was redesigned once again, and the lights are now better integrated into the wings. Colours are metallic blue, red, and cream.
Price guide: £250
(Courtesy Bruce Sterling)

Diapet D167 Mercedes-Benz 220S

As with the Volkswagen, Diapet fitted an opening boot and bonnet to the original Cherryca casting. Colours are red, cream or black.
Price guide: £200
(Courtesy Bruce Sterling)

Diapet D165 Volkswagen

First seen as Cherryca Phenix PHE8, the Volkswagen Beetle was reworked by Diapet and given an opening boot and bonnet. However, the two versions do not look the same as the wheels of the Diapet are smaller, making it 'sit' differently. Colour choices on the Diapet are metallic light blue, red or cream.
Price guide: £200
(Courtesy Bruce Sterling)

Diapet D113 Datsun Fairlady Convertible

The three German cars shown above are not 'typical' Diapet subjects; the vast majority were based on Japanese vehicles. The 1960 Datsun Fairlady first appeared as Cherryca Phenix PHE16 (left), but the Diapet version (right) looks like a new casting and has an opening bonnet.
Price guide: £200
(Courtesy Bruce Sterling)

JAPAN

Diapet D119 Prince Gloria

The Prince Gloria was later renamed as a Nissan after the two companies merged in 1966. It first appeared in model form as Cherryca Phenix PHE24, and the Diapet issue appears to be the same apart from the baseplate.
Price guide: £200
(Courtesy Bruce Sterling)

Diapet D129 Toyopet Crown Police Patrol Car

The Crown was Toyota's flagship model and is not unlike the Prince Gloria in appearance. This Diapet is based on Cherryca Phenix PHE26 and was available both as an ordinary saloon and in this black and white police livery with plastic accessories – a roof light and bonnet siren or searchlight.
Price guide: £200
(Courtesy Bruce Sterling)

Diapet D131 Honda S600 Convertible

The Honda S600 was so small and light that it managed to reach a top speed of 90mph in spite of having an engine capacity of only 600cc. As the real car did not appear until March 1964, the Cherryca Phenix model of it (PHE 38) could not have been in production for very long, which explains why it is incredibly rare. The Diapet version seems to be just as hard to find.
Price guide: £400
(Courtesy Bruce Sterling)

Diapet D151 Toyota Crown Station Wagon

Cherryca Phenix PHE27 was a Toyota Crown Station Wagon which Diapet transformed into an ambulance. But it made another version as well – a red and yellow promotional issue for the Tokyo Shibaura Electric Co Inc, better known as Toshiba. Released in 1966, the door script is written in Arabic which has led to suggestions that it was made for export to Iran. This is by far the rarest Diapet and arguably the rarest Japanese diecast of all time.
Price guide: £1000+
(Courtesy Bruce Sterling)

Diapet D153 Toyota Publica

A simple diecast model of the Publica, without opening parts, had already appeared in the Model Pet range. The Diapet, though an entirely new casting, still has the typical Cherryca Phenix finish with bare metal showing through to create the effect of chrome round the windows, bumpers and grille.
Price guide: £175
(Courtesy Bruce Sterling)

Diapet D162 Toyota 2000GT

With the 2000GT, Toyota made Japan's first serious attempt to rival European sports cars. Only 337 examples were produced in the three years between 1967 and 1970. Doors and bonnet open but, as on many early Diapets, these parts do not fit very well. The model was available in the three colours used for several other Diapets: cream, red, and metallic blue.
Price guide: £175
(Courtesy Bruce Sterling)

Diapet D164 Nissan Gloria

This model represents another generation of the large Gloria saloon, badged as a Nissan after 1966. The Diapet is made in the same style as the previous model (D119) with plenty of exposed metal 'chrome' detailing.
Price guide: £200
(Courtesy Bruce Sterling)

Diapet D169 Honda S800 Convertible

In 1966, Honda replaced the S600 with the larger-engined S800, although visually the cars were very similar. Diapet's model now had opening doors and boot, as well as the opening bonnet fitted to the S600.
Price guide: £400
(Courtesy Bruce Sterling)

JAPAN

Diapet D166 Mazda Cosmo Sport

Produced between 1967 and 1972, the Cosmo was Mazda's first rotary-engined car. The Diapet model dates from 1968 and, while still rare and desirable, was no longer made using the Cherryca Phenix antimony method; it has a conventional diecast body with separate components for the front and rear bumpers. Soon, all new Diapet releases were made in the same way, and the range lost a degree of distinctiveness as a result. The Cosmo is also available in black and white police livery.
Price guide: £200
(Courtesy Bruce Sterling)

Diapet D149 Porsche 911

While specialising in Japanese cars, Diapet never completely lost interest in European vehicles, and three other original models were made using the antimony method. The Porsche 911 dates from 1964 and the thinking behind it was to produce a faster and more comfortable successor to the 356, which had been based on the Volkswagen Beetle. As on most other Diapets, doors, bonnet and boot open, and the colour choices are – yet again – metallic light blue, red or cream.
Price guide: £175
(Courtesy Bruce Sterling)

Diapet D157 Volkswagen 1600

In 1961 Volkswagen launched the 1500 saloon which led, five years later, to the fastback-styled 1600, familiar to collectors in model form thanks to the Dinky Toy and Matchbox replicas. The Diapet is not quite as well-proportioned as the Dinky, but is, of course, much rarer.
Price guide: £175
(Courtesy Bruce Sterling)

Diapet D175 Fiat 850 Spider

The rear-engined Fiat 850 was an evolution of the popular Fiat 600, and the 850 Spyder was in turn developed out of the saloon. It appeared in 1965 with stylish bodywork designed by Bertone. The Diapet model has an opening bonnet and boot, and sits well with other similar convertibles in the series, such as the Honda S800 and Datsun Fairlady.
Price guide: £175
(Courtesy Bruce Sterling)

108

Diecast cars have been made in some of the most unlikely corners of the globe. Often redundant tooling from European manufacturers was sold on and used in less economically developed countries, though many small ranges of original models were also produced in unexpected locations, some of them of remarkably high quality. In the space available it is obviously impossible to give a comprehensive survey of all world diecasts; instead, this chapter will focus on a few of the manufacturers whose histories are reasonably well documented.

Argentina: Buby

The Buby range from Argentina was one of the few from that part of the world that matched the quality of European diecasts. 'Buby' was the childhood nickname of an engineer called Harold Mahler, and he used this as a trademark for the model cars that he began to manufacture at the family home, having been introduced to die-casting technology by one of his professors at the University of Buenos Aires. The first two subjects chosen were a 1957 Buick Station Wagon and a 1958 Ford Fairlane, consisting of a solid, one-piece casting with the windows sprayed silver rather than cut out. These early issues are very rare because they often suffer from metal fatigue. However, quality quickly improved on later models.

Most model car ranges reflect the kind of vehicles to be seen on the roads of the country where they were made, and Buby was no exception. Over the years, for example, several different versions of the Ford Falcon were modelled – understandably enough, as Ford assembled this car at its Pacheco plant, 38 kilometres outside Buenos Aires. Starting in 1962, production of the Falcon continued until 1991, by which time nearly half a million examples had been built.

Similarly, the American Kaiser Manhattan was built at a factory in the province of Cordoba by Industrias Kaiser Argentina (IKA). Sadly for American car fans, Buby never modelled the Manhattan, known locally as the Kaiser Carabela, but other vehicles made in the IKA plant, such as the Jeep-based Estanciera station wagon and the later Rambler-based Torino, were included in the Buby range. Renaults, Peugeots and Fiats were all assembled in Argentina, too, hence the presence of cars like the Dauphine, Peugeot 504 and Fiat 1500, 125 and 128 in the Buby lineup. No diecast range would be complete without a Volkswagen Beetle, and this is one of Buby's most sought-after models. One or two more exotic choices crept in, too, such as a Mercedes 300 sports and a Porsche Carrera 6.

From the collector's point of view, the Buby series peaked in the mid-1960s. Thereafter, like so many other diecast ranges, unrealistic wheels and garish stickers began to detract from their appeal. In any case, children preferred the smaller-scale Hot Wheels and Matchbox-size cars, with the result that Buby jumped on this bandwagon, too. Some interesting cars were chosen, like the Peugeot 404, Citroën Ami 8 estate car, the ubiquitous Ford Falcon, and the Citroën 3CV (Citroën assembled the 2CV in Argentina, and when a larger engine was fitted in the later 1960s, the model was designated a 3CV). The small Buby cars were still in production in the 1990s, and in recent years Buby has branched out into the more expensive handbuilt market with the 'Collectors' Classics' series of 1950s American cars.

Buby may be the most extensive range of models to be made in Argentina, but it was by no means the only one. Clau-mar made a series of 1/50 scale buses, while Galgo offered some simple diecasts in about 1/35-1/40 scale, of interest mainly because one of them was a Ford Taunus, yet another European car to be assembled in South America. A series of Hot Wheels lookalikes was made under the unflattering title of 'Muky,' while Aguti made some acceptable Matchbox-type cars in the late 1970s, among them a VW Beetle, Morris 1100, and Mini Cooper.

Israel: Gamda and Sabra

Gamda toys were made in Kibbutz Kfar Hanassi, Israel, from ex-River Series moulds (see page 12) in the early 1960s. The vehicles represented dated from a decade earlier but Gamda did its best to improve the finish with two-tone paintwork, 'chrome' wheels, and window glazing. The words 'made in England' on the base were replaced by 'Made in Israel,' and the cars were packed in generic black and yellow boxes carrying the Gamda name and address in Hebrew on one face and in English on the other. Some of the less realistic River Series trucks were also used by Gamda and issued in liveries that related to their Israeli context, such as 'Tnuva' Dairies

8115/1 – Israeli Police Car
4-3/4 in. (120 mm)
With openable trunk

POLICE

**Exclusive Models !
Israeli Die-Cast Cars.**

8101/1 –
Israeli Magen David Ambulance
4-1/4 in. (110 mm)
With swinging rear door

8107/1 – Israeli Tourist Bureau Car

4-1/2 in. (115 mm)
With openable trunk

8100/4 – Israeli Postal Service Car

Length: 4-3/8 in. (110 mm)
With swinging rear door

These catalogue pages show how the Sabra range catered for both domestic and export markets. While the subjects were predominantly American cars, many appear with local Israeli liveries.

and a tanker with 'Sonol,' 'Delek' or 'Paz' markings. Nearly a third of Gamda models represented military vehicles, a reflection of the volatile political situation in the Middle East. In a similar vein, the military Jeep and tanker appeared in white liveries with United Nations lettering, as vehicles with UN markings would be easily recognisable on the home market.

However, not every Gamda model was derived from a River Series casting. The Bedford covered truck is a copy or reissue of a similar model by another minor English maker, Kemlow – itself a copy of a Dinky Toys item. Two of Gamda's best models were original castings: a single deck Leyland Worldmaster bus, available in two-tone blue and grey, or in three-tone El-Al airlines colours (blue, white and green). There is also a realistic station wagon based on a Willys Jeep, available as a panel van, ambulance or dark blue and white police car.

Although these toys sold well on the local market, by 1965 it had become clear to Gamda's parent company, Habonim, that production was not sustainable and Gamda seemed doomed to extinction. Michael Cohen of Kibbutz Kfar Hanassi, a key figure in the toy manufacturing project, sums up the problem as follows: "Although the toy models were very popular, we did not see any profits from the venture, mainly because this kind of business demands high volume production, much higher than the Israeli market could absorb. On the other hand, we could not see ourselves breaking into the international market with the kind of models we had, especially as firms like Matchbox were at the height of their success."[1]

Then one of Israel's largest industrial companies, Koor, made an approach as it had a customer interested in placing an order for a completely new series of model cars. The customer in question was Cragstan, a major New York toy distributor. Cragstan wanted to enter the 1/43 diecast market and placed an order for three million cars – sold as 'Detroit Seniors' in the USA, and as 'Sabra' in other export markets. The new range was primarily aimed at the American market as all but one of the twenty models of road cars were based on US prototypes. Gamda was quite creative in devising alternative liveries to produce 'new' models, so that there are actually around 50 different Sabras to collect – not only the usual police, fire and taxi variations but models with Hebrew lettering such as the 'Magen David' ambulance, UN vehicles and Israeli presidential cars. Some Sabras carry decorations that reflect the crazes of the period, notably a Volkswagen and Dodge Charger covered in flowers representing the 'Hippy' era!

Compared to the earlier Gamdas, the Sabras are more modern in appearance and construction, with opening parts and much use of plastic for interiors and baseplates. The range is significant as relatively few late 1960s American cars were modelled by other manufacturers, and American car collectors are grateful to Sabra for providing models of cars such as the Chevrolet Chevelle Station Wagon, Chevrolet Impala, Pontiac GTO, Plymouth Valiant and Chrysler Imperial Cabriolet.

India: Maxwell and Milton

A similar pattern can be discerned in the Indian diecast industry: at first old tooling from Dinky, Matchbox and Corgi was used, with original models following later. The main names here are Nicky Toys, Maxwell, and Milton of Calcutta. Starting in 1968, Dinky sold the moulds for old models to India where they re-emerged crudely finished, with poor quality wheels that are often too small. Sometimes the Nicky Toys boxes still retained the 'Dinky' logo, with the letters 'D' and 'n' having been quickly changed by pen to 'N' and 'c' respectively. Surprisingly, though, some of these Indian issues are now quite sought-after by collectors. Among the original designs, it is worth singling out the Maxwell model of the Hindustan Ambassador which has been a familiar sight on Indian roads for many years. Many Indian toys were recycled British diecasts; in the same way, the Hindustan was basically a 1950s Morris Oxford!

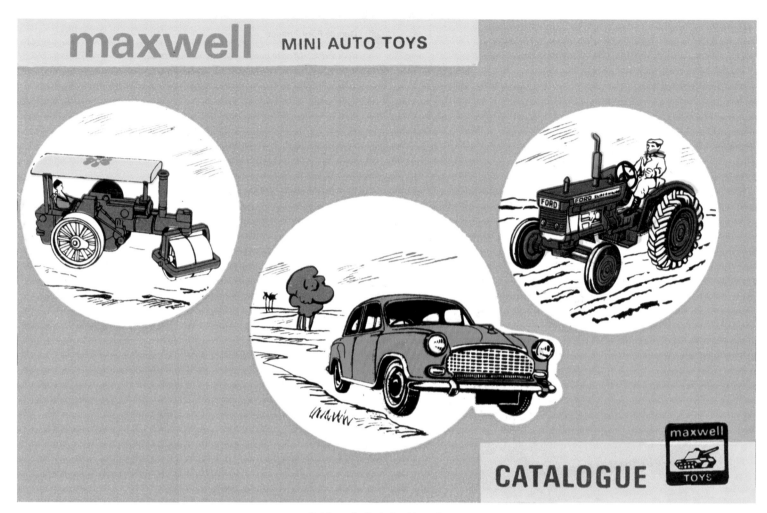

Catalogue for the Indian Maxwell range.

Australia and New Zealand: Micro Models and Fun Ho!

The history of Micro Models is complex and involved, beginning around 1952 in Melbourne with a series of models in 1/43 scale. Australia's membership of the British Commonwealth ensured that a good number of British vehicles were included, the Standard Vanguard Estate car, Humber Super Snipe, and Vauxhall Cresta being particularly appreciated by collectors. However, Micro's key contribution to diecast history was to make available models of Australian cars like the Holden FX and FJ van.

Sometime in the mid-1950s Micro moulds were also used by Lincoln Industries of New Zealand. Although Micro Model production in Australia did not continue into the 1960s, the moulds survived and models have subsequently been reissued on more than one occasion. Collectors need to take great care when purchasing Micro Models items as something that may appear to be a 1950s original could, in fact, be a much later reissue.

Meanwhile, in New Zealand, HJ Underwood started to make toys in 1939, selling them under the unusual trademark of 'Fun Ho!' (always with an exclamation mark). Initially these were hollow-cast from lead, and later aluminium. However, the brand is best known for a range of Matchbox-sized diecast models produced between 1962 and 1982. Rather like the British Morestone 'Esso' series, Fun Ho! secured a promotional deal with the Mobil oil company.

The history of Fun Ho! is well-documented, and there is considerable interest in the brand in New Zealand today. The Fun Ho! museum at Inglewood, Taranaki, offers replicas of some of the earlier models, which are still being made from the original moulds. Full details can be found on the website www.funho.com.

[1] Extract from a letter to the author.

THE REST OF THE WORLD

Gamda Ford Prefect
The Prefect was a very popular family car in Britain in the 1950s, but comparatively few models of it have been made. The Gamda model uses ex-River Series tooling (see page 12).
Price guide: £175

Gamda Buick
Gamda greatly improved on the plain River Series model by adding window glazing, two-tone paint, and chrome wheels. The model resembles a 1953 prototype.
Price guide: £175

Gamda Daimler Conquest
Finished in a very suitable two-tone grey, this model of the 6-cylinder 2.5 litre Daimler is the best of the Gamda cars.
Price guide: £200

Gamda Daimler Conquest
This hitherto unrecorded colour variation in blue and grey is believed to be a colour trial that did not reach the stage of production. Note the later grey plastic wheels compared to the chrome hubs on the standard version.
Price guide: £350+
(Courtesy Gary Cohen)

Gamda Tnuva Dairies van

Although it does not represent an exact prototype, this truck is of interest as it was issued in an Israeli livery with both English and Hebrew lettering.
Price guide: £300+

Gamda Bedford Driving School truck

Not every Gamda was derived from a River Series casting. This Bedford resembles the British Kemlows model – which itself was closely based on a Dinky Toy.
Price guide: £250+
(Courtesy Douglas R Kelly)

Gamda UN Tanker

This articulated tanker appeared in a number of different liveries.
Price guide: £200+
(Courtesy Gary Cohen)

Gamda Bus

The Leyland Worldmaster bus is one of the few completely original castings in the Gamda range. It is based on a prototype used by Egged, the national Israeli bus company, and also exists in a rare variation in the livery of El-Al airlines.
Price guide: £200; El-Al: £350

THE REST OF THE WORLD

Gamda Massey-Ferguson Tractor
One of the rarest and most realistic Gamdas, this tractor looks very similar to the Corgi model which was introduced in 1959.
Price guide: £250+
(Courtesy Gary Cohen)

Gamda Israel Defence Army Set
A scarce set containing a selection of Gamda military vehicles. A tank transporter made from an ex-Kemlows casting also exists.
Price guide: £400 +
(Courtesy Gary Cohen)

Sabra 8117 Volkswagen
This model served as the basis of numerous variations: Swiss PTT, Deutsche Bundespost, Polizei, and even a 'hippy' car decorated with flowers!
Price guide: £30

Sabra 8116 Chevrolet Impala Taxi
The Impala also came in two police liveries, one of them an Israeli patrol car designed to appeal to the local market.
Price guide: £25

Sabra 8100/1 Chevrolet Chevelle Station Wagon 'UN'
At least eleven different colour and livery variations of the Chevelle Station Wagon have been identified, several of them representing vehicles that would have been familiar in Israel, such as this United Nations model.
Price guide: £25

Sabra 8111 Chrysler Imperial Convertible and 8106/1 Ford Mustang
Two more Sabra American cars. Note the seventies-style 'psychedelic' decoration on the Mustang!
Price guide: £25 each

Buby 1002 Ford Fairlane
The second model in the Buby series was this 1958 Ford Fairlane (the first being a 1957 Buick). The Ford is to 1/40 scale and can be found either with solid silver-painted windows or with conventional plastic glazing.
Price guide: £300+
(Courtesy Gary Cohen)

Buby 1003 Ford Fairlane Policia
In addition to the civilian version, the Fairlane comes in rally or 'Policia' guise. The survival rate of early Buby models is low as many suffered from metal fatigue.
Price guide: £300+
(Courtesy Gary Cohen)

THE REST OF THE WORLD

Buby 1004 Ford Pick-up
Based on a 1957 American Ford F-100, this model also comes in military livery and as a breakdown truck. Scale is stated as 1/40.
Price guide: £250

Buby 1006 Ford Wrecker truck
This variation of the Ford F-100 is in the livery of the 'Automovil Club Argentino.'
Price guide: £250
(Courtesy Gary Cohen)

Buby 1005 VW
One of the best and most sought-after early Buby diecasts, this 1/40 scale Volkswagen Beetle features window glazing and suspension.
Price guide: £200

Buby 1012 Mercedes-Benz 220SE
A well-proportioned model of the popular Mercedes 220SE in 1/43 scale. It also comes with rally markings.
Price guide: £175
(Courtesy Gary Cohen)

Dinky (Hong Kong) 002 Chevrolet Corvair Monza

One of a group of six American cars produced in Hong Kong for Dinky Toys between 1965 and 1967 with the US market in mind. The others were: 001 Buick Riviera, 003 Chevrolet Impala, 004 Dodge Polara, 005 Ford Thunderbird and 006 Rambler Classic Station Wagon.
Price guide: £120

Lincoln (Hong Kong) Ford Timber truck

A hefty eight-inch long truck made entirely from metal, except for the timber load that is in fact a single block of wood with lines scored along it to represent planks. This is quite a cosmopolitan toy: not only is it an American truck made in Hong Kong, but it was distributed in Europe by Lincoln International, a toy distributor of the 1960s originally based in New Zealand.
Price guide: £40

Micro Models Chrysler Royal Sedan
Based on a 1956 prototype, this model was made in Australia and can be found in numerous colours.
Price guide: £100
(Courtesy Gary Cohen)

Streamlux Holden
An Australian company which manufactured products such as electrical components made a very small quantity of these 1/36 scale Holden sedans in 1957. Some twenty years later, the original tooling was reused and a further 1000 examples produced, distributed in kit form by an Australian toy dealer.
Price guide: £90
(Picture and background information courtesy Douglas R Kelly)

THE REST OF THE WORLD

Fun-Ho! 18 Austin Articulated Truck

Just under 3 inches in length, this model was produced in New Zealand between 1966 and 1972 and can be found with both painted or chrome-plated finish.
Price guide: £30
(Courtesy Douglas R Kelly)

Nicky Toys 137 Plymouth Fury Sports

Tooling for the 1963 Dinky Toys model of the Plymouth later went to India, where the car was issued as part of the Nicky Toys range in this metallic green shade.
Price guide: £65
(Courtesy Gary Cohen)

Maxwell 510 Hindustan Ambassador

Let down by its poor quality wheels, this item is, nevertheless, of interest as it represents a popular Indian car which was based on a 1950s Morris Oxford.
(Courtesy Douglas R Kelly)
Price guide: £25

Marx (Hong Kong) Volkswagen

In the late 1960s/early 1970s, Marx made some simple, Matchbox-size cars in Hong Kong. The range also included a Jaguar E Type.
Price guide: £8

APPENDIX 1:
MANUFACTURERS OF DIECAST TOY CARS

NOTES:
1. Dates refer to the start of diecast production and not to the year that the company was founded, as many toy companies made other products as well as diecast cars. Often, only an approximate date can be given.
2. Few diecast toy ranges were made to a consistent scale. Unless otherwise indicated, toys are in the 1/40-1/50 range (about 4-5 inches in length). The terms 'small-scale' or 'Matchbox-sized' cover models in the 1/64-1/90 range (about 2.5-3 inches in length).

Brand name	Country of origin	Approx. date	Comments
AHI	USA	1960s	US distributor of toys made in Japan, including sets of small-scale diecast vehicles.
All American	USA	1947	Based in Salem, Oregon. Maker of large (1 inch to the foot) robust trucks.
AR	France	1920s	One of the earliest recorded diecast ranges.
Arbur	GB	1946	London-based maker of a small number of diecast vehicles.
Arro	GB	c.1948	Maker of an Austin Seven racer and a Commer van.
Asahi (ATC)	Japan	1959	Maker of Model Pet, the first 1/43 series to specialise in models of Japanese cars.
Automec	UK	1956	Based in Lincoln, England. Short-lived diecast range, mostly Bedford trucks.
Barclay	USA	1924	Based in New Jersey, Barclay made many lead-alloy vehicles before World War II. Small-scale diecasts, known as the 'Bottle Series,' were made in the 1960s.
Benbros	UK	1954	A range of small Matchbox-style models, originally called the TV Series and later Mighty Midgets.
Best Box	Holland	1970s	A series of Matchbox-sized cars, later know as Efsi.
Birk	Denmark	c.1935	Some of the 'Metallo' series by KA Birk and Co of Copenhagen were copies of American Tootsietoys.
Bradscar	UK	1950s	A small series of British cars made as OO gauge railway accessories.
Brent	Australia	1950s	Diecast cars and trucks.
Brimtoy	UK	1950s	Some diecast vehicles, though most Brimtoys were made of tinplate and/or plastic.
Britains	UK	1932	Famous maker of toy soldiers. Numerous vehicles were also made pre and postwar.
Brosol	Brazil	1968	Distributed Solido Toys in Brazil but also made a few original models, notably a Volkswagen 1200.
Budgie	UK	1959	Commercial vehicle models and some Matchbox-sized cars.
Buby	Argentina	1957	Diecast cars in various scales.
Camcast	USA	1950s	Simple delivery vans in a variety of advertising liveries.
CD	France	1920s	Early diecast brand which made numerous Renault models.
Chad Valley	UK	1950s	Series of clockwork-powered model cars, mostly based on Rootes Group vehicles.
Charbens	UK	1930s	Large range of metal toy vehicles, some of them horse-drawn.

APPENDIX 1

Brand name	Country of origin	Approx. date	Comments
Cherryca Phenix	Japan	1962	Successor to Taiseiya's Micro Pet series (see below). Range consisted of Japanese, American and European cars.
CIJ	France	1950	Extensive series of diecast cars, particularly Renaults.
Collectoy	Japan	1958	Models of American cars and European sports cars, made by CK (Kuramochi) in Japan for Marx who also distributed them under the Linemar name.
Corgi Toys	UK	1956	Extensive range of diecast vehicles of all types.
Dalia	Spain	1933	Spanish distributor of French Solido toys and manufacturer of diecast cars and motor scooters.
DCMT	UK		[See Lone Star]
Diapet	Japan	1965	Diecast cars, many of them based on Japanese prototypes.
Dinky Toys	UK/France	1934	Extensive range of diecast vehicles of all types, made in factories at Binns Road, Liverpool, England and Bobigny, France.
Diti Toys	Israel	1960s	Copies or reissues of Morestone commercial vehicles.
Dugu	Italy	1963	Veteran and vintage cars.
Ediltoys	Italy	1970	Small range of 1/43 scale cars.
Efsi	Holland	1970s	Successor to Best Box.
Eria	France	1957	A small range of diecast cars, distributed in chain stores under the name 'Punch.'
Faracars	France	1960s	1/43 scale Indianapolis racing car.
France Jouets (FJ)	France	1959	1/50 scale commercial vehicles.
Fun Ho!	New Zealand	1962	Diecast cars in various scales.
Gama	Germany	1959	'Minimod' series.
Gamda	Israel	1960s	Diecast cars and trucks, mostly from ex-River Series moulds.
Gasquy	Belgium	late 1940s	Very rare series of cars including a Tatra and Studebaker.
Gitanes	France	1950s	Small-scale diecast cars.
Goodee	USA	1950s	Simple vehicles in Tootsietoy style.
Grafil	Argentina	1960s	Manufacturer of a Volkswagen delivery van.
Guisval	Spain	1960s	Diecast cars in various scales.
Gulliver	France	1940s	Small range of vehicles made of aluminium.
Hot Wheels	USA	1968	Cars with low-friction wheels made by Mattel.
Hubley	USA	1936	Extensive range of diecast toys in various scales.
Husky	UK	1964	Matchbox-size models from the maker of Corgi.
Impy	UK	1965	A range of 3-inch diecasts featuring opening parts, made by Lone Star. Known as Flyers from 1969 on.
Jadali	France	1950s	Small diecast vehicles copied from Lesney's Matchbox series.
Jadali	Spain	1950s	Metamol of Barcelona issued a diecast Seat 1400 under the Jadali name. It is not known whether there is any connection with French Jadali toys.
Jefe	Spain	1950s	Lion Cars for the Spanish market.
Joal	Spain	1968	Range of 1/43 diecasts, some made from tooling bought from other companies.
Jolly Roger	UK	1947	Diecast cars made in Wales.
JRD	France	c. 1956	Specialised in Citroën models.
Kembo	UK	c.1948	Made some Scammell diecast trucks and a police car.

MANUFACTURERS OF DIECAST TOY CARS

Brand name	Country of origin	Approx. date	Comments
Kemlows	UK	1946	North London diecasting firm founded by Charles Kempster and William Lowe.
Lemeco	Sweden	1950s	Several diecast cars, similar to Dinky Toys.
Lenyko	Sweden	1950s	Made one model only, a Volvo PV444.
Lesney	UK	1947	Best known for Matchbox models, though other, larger diecasts preceded these.
Les Rouliers	France	1950s	Matchbox-sized models of trucks and construction equipment.
Lincoln	New Zealand	1950s	Various diecasts originally made by other companies also appeared under the Lincoln name (e.g. River Series). A small-scale series was also issued, originally called 'Matchbox Series' until Lesney objected and the name was changed to 'Motorway Mini Series.' The history of this range was traced in detail in an article by Robert Newson in *Diecast Collector* magazine, April 1999.
Lion Car	Holland	1956	Specialised in models of Daf cars and trucks.
London Toy	Canada and USA	1940s	Simple diecast vehicles.
Lone Star	UK	1956	Various ranges of model cars were made by DCMT (Die Casting Machine Tools Ltd). Scales ranged from 1/35 (early Road-master series) to 1/118 (Tuf Tots trucks).
Majorette	France	1965	Large range of small-scale cars.
Manoil	USA	1934	Various cars and trucks.
Märklin	Germany	1930s	Various pre and postwar ranges of diecast cars.
Marusan	Japan	1950s	A small series of commercial vehicles, mostly based on British and French Dinky Toys.
Marx	Hong Kong	1950s	Mainly tinplate and plastic toys, but some diecasts were made.
Masudaya	Japan	1950s	Silver Pet series of American cars with chrome plated finish.
Matchbox	UK	1953	Very successful series of small-scale diecast cars made by the Lesney company.
Maxwell	India	1970s	Series of poorly finished diecasts, mostly made from second-hand tooling.
Mebetoys	Italy	1966	1/43 scale diecast cars, later taken over by Mattel.
Meboto	Turkey	1970s	Reissue of Italian Edil Toy castings.
Mecline	Norway	1956	Distributed Danish Tekno models under licence in Norway between 1956 and 1960.
Mercury	Italy	1945	Founded in Turin in 1932, Mercury was the biggest diecast brand in Italy before Politoys.
Metallo	Denmark	1930s	Model cars similar in style to American Tootsietoys.
Metosul	Portugal	1965	Models mostly based on Corgi, Gama, Dinky and other makes.
Mettoy	UK	1948	Parent company of Corgi Toys. Made some large scale diecasts prior to 1956 under the Castoys name.
Micromodels	Australia	c.1952	Cars and trucks, notably Australian Holdens. Also made in New Zealand.
Micro Pet	Japan	1961	Series of model cars made by the Taiseiya company.
Midgetoys	USA	1946	Diecast vehicles similar in style to Tootsietoys.
Midget Toys	France	1950s	Small-scale diecast vehicles.
Milton	India	1960s/70s	Poorly finished diecasts, some made from ex-Dinky tooling.
Miniature Pet	Japan	1962	Only one model is known: a 1958 Opel Kapitan.
Möbius	Germany	1950s	Small range of racing car models.
Morestone	UK	1948	Diecast vehicles, some of them horse-drawn. Forerunner of Budgie Toys.
Nacoral	Spain	1967	1/43 cars in plastic and later in diecast metal.
Nicky Toys	India	1970s	Crudely made reissues from ex-Dinky Toy moulds.
Norev	France	1971	Extensive range of plastic and, from 1971 onwards, diecast cars.
Penny Toys	Italy	1967	Small-scale series by Politoys (see below).
Pilen	Spain	1960s	1/43 scale cars.
Politoys	Italy	1965	Plastic cars from 1960 onwards; 1/43 diecast range launched in 1965.
Prämeta	Germany	1950s	Small series of mechanical cars varying in size from 1/30 to 1/40 scale.

APPENDIX 1

Brand name	Country of origin	Approx. date	Comments
Quiralu	France	c.1956	Small 1/43 range.
Ralstoy	USA	1950s	Early products were mostly articulated trucks. Later the company produced simple vans for use as advertising promotionals.
RAMI	France	1958	Vintage cars.
Ra-Ro	Italy	1940s	Made four diecast racing cars.
Rex	Germany	1960s	Ford Thunderbird and Opel Kapitan in 1/42 scale.
Rio	Italy	1962	Specialised in veteran and vintage vehicles.
River Series	UK	1950s	Simple cars and trucks, some with friction motors.
Robin Hood	UK	1940s	Simple diecast cars and trucks.
Rolytoys	Brazil	c.1968	Small range of Matchbox-size diecasts.
RW Modell	Germany	1963	1/43 scale diecasts.
Sablon	Belgium	1968	Short-lived range of 1/43 scale cars.
Sabra	Israel	1967	Mostly American cars in 1/43 from the makers of Gamda.
Safir	France	1960s	Veteran cars and Champion series of racing cars.
Salza	France	1960s	Specialised in models of vehicles associated with the Tour de France cycle race.
Schuco	Germany	1950s	Numerous different diecast ranges.
Sentry Box	UK	1950s	Series of Matchbox-size military vehicles by Kemlows.
Shackleton	UK	1948	Large-scale Foden lorries.
Siku	Germany	1963	Produced plastic toys in the 1950s and introduced diecast cars in 1963.
Slik Toy	USA	c.1946	Maker of aluminium and plastic cars and tractors, based in Lansing, Iowa.
Solido	France	1930s	Introduced a series of 'Automobiles à Transformation' in the 1930s and the more realistic 1/43 scale 100 series in 1957.
Spot-On	UK	1959	Diecast vehicles and accessories in 1/42 scale. Made by Tri-ang. Production of some models continued in New Zealand after 1967.
SR	France	1920s	Very early French diecast range, including a Ford Model T.
Streamlux	Australia	1950s	Small-scale diecasts. The moulds were sold to Underwood of New Zealand who reissued them as Fun Ho!
Sundaw	UK	1950s	Single and double deck bus models.
Tekno	Denmark	1940s	High quality diecast models.
Timpo	UK	1940s	Simple, heavy diecast toy vehicles.
Tomica	Japan	1970	Three-inch diecasts. Later, the 1/43 scale Tomica Dandy series was launched.
Tootsietoys	USA	1911	Regarded as the pioneer of diecast cars.
TTI	GB	1950s	Based in Stoke-on-Trent. Two very simple diecast cars are known.
Tuf Tots	UK	1969	Range of small 'pocket money' diecast cars made by Lone Star.
Tutsitoys	Mexico	1970s	Reissues of American Tootsietoys.
Vilmer	Denmark	1950s	An extensive range of trucks and a small number of cars.
Winross	USA	1960s	American advertising promotional trucks.
Zax	Italy	1940s	Based in Bergamo. Made simple diecasts after World War Two.
Zebra Toys	GB	1960s	Diecast series from Benbros, larger in scale than the company's Mighty Midget series.
Ziss	Germany	1960s	Veteran cars made by RW Modell.

APPENDIX 2:
BIBLIOGRAPHY

Books

Ambridge, Geoffrey S
The Bumper Book of Lone Star Diecast Models and Toys, 1948-88
(Privately printed, 2002)

Azema, Bertrand
Jouets Solido 1932-1957
(Editions EPA, Paris, 1991)

Azema, Bertrand
Jouets Solido 1957-1991
(Editions EPA, Paris, 1991)

Beaujardin, Didier, et al
Le Monde fantastique de Norev
(Editions Grancher, Paris, 2005)

Brooks, Paul and Jennifer
Automec: A Brief History
(Privately printed, 2006) See www.mastermodels.org.uk

Brousse, Lucien
Buby: La Historia en Fotos
(Privately published, Argentina, 1999)

Brown, Kenneth D.
Factory of Dreams: a History of Meccano Ltd
(Crucible Books, Lancaster, 2007)

Cordes, Peter R
Modellauto Katalog 1:43 [history of 1/43 scale German diecast ranges]
(Alba, Düsseldorf, Germany, 1985)

Dujardin, Jacques
The Dinky Toys Encyclopedia (CD rom)
(dinkycollect@free.fr)

Duprat, Mick
Les Jouets Renault [covers history of diecast Renaults by CIJ]
(Rétroviseur, Paris, 1994)

Force, Edward
Classic Miniature Vehicles Made in France
(Schiffer Publishing, Pennsylvania, USA, 1991)
Force, Edward
Classic Miniature Vehicles of Northern Europe
(Schiffer Publishing, Pennsylvania, USA, 2002)

Gibson, Cecil
A History of British Dinky Toys 1934-1964
(Model Aeronautical Press, Hemel Hempstead, 1966)

Hermans, Marc
Encyclopédie des Jouets et Miniatures Citroën
(Rétroviseur, Paris, 1995)

Houchangnia, Fabian
Käfer Miniaturen: Alle Modelle von 1935 bis 1957 [Volkswagen Beetle models]
(Delius Klasing, Bielefeld, Germany, 2008)

Huber, Rudger
Schuco Piccolo
(Battenberg, Augsburg, Germany, 1998)

Johansen, Dorte and Hedegård, Hans
Danske Modelbiler [Danish Model Cars]
(SamlerBørsen, Copenhagen, Denmark, 2002)

Johansen, Dorte and Hedegård, Hans
Tekno
(Tøgborsen, Copenhagen, Denmark, 1984)

APPENDIX 2

Kelly, Douglas R.
Die Cast Price Guide Postwar: 1946-Present
(Antique Trader Books, Dubuque, Iowa, USA, 1997)

McGimpsey, Kevin and Orr, Stewart
Collecting Matchbox Diecast Toys: the first forty years
(Major Productions, Chester, 1989)

Moro, Philippe
Hep! Taxi [A photographic record of model taxis from all over the world]
(Editions Drivers, Toulouse, France, 2005)

Nakajima, Noboru
Model Cars of the World
(Hoikusha Publishing, Osaka, Japan, 1977)

Newson, Robert
Benbros TV Series and Mighty Midgets
(privately printed, 2002)

Newson, Robert
Budgie Models
(Leisure Time Publications, Suffolk, 1988)

O'Brien, Richard
Collecting Toy Cars and Trucks
(Krause Publications, Iola, Wisconsin, USA, 1997)

Ralston, Andrew G
Toy Cars of Japan and Hong Kong
(Schiffer Publishing, Atglen, Pennsylvania, USA, 2001)

Rampini, Paolo
The Golden Book of Model Cars, 1900-1975
(edizioni Paolo Rampini, Milan, Italy 1995)

Ramsay, John (ed)
British Diecast Model Toys Catalogue 12th edition
(Warners Group Publications, Bourne, 2007)

Redempt, Thierry and Ferrer, Pierre
Les Jouets CIJ en Zamac
(Editions Drivers, Toulouse, France, 2006)

Richardson, Mike and Sue
Dinky Toys and Modelled Miniatures
(New Cavendish Books, London, 1981)

Richardson, Mike and Sue
The Great Book of Dinky Toys
(New Cavendish Books, London, 2000)

Roulet, Jean-Michel
Histoire des Dinky Toys Français, 1933-78
(Editions Adepte, Paris, 1978)

Tobbe, Hans et al.
Lion Car 1956-1981
(Automobilia Collection, Overveen, Holland, 1981)

Trench, Patrick
Model Cars and Road Vehicles
(Pelham Books, London, 1983)

van Cleemput, Marcel
The Great Book of Corgi, 1956-1983
(New Cavendish Books, London, 1989)

Wieland, James and Force, Edward
Tootsietoys: World's First Diecast Models
(Motorbooks International, Osceola, Wisconsin, USA, 1980)

Wieland, James and Force, Edward
Detroit in Minature
(Miniature Auto Sales, Litchfield, Connecticut, USA, 1983)

Zarnock, Michael
Hot Wheels Variations: the Ultimate Guide
(Krause Publications, USA, 2007)

Zarnock, Michael and Van Bogart, Angelo
Warman's Hot Wheels Field Guide
(Krause Publications, USA, 2007)

MAGAZINE WEBSITES

A number of excellent magazines exist which contain detailed articles on individual manufacturers, themes and model variations. These magazines are also a useful source of addresses of specialist dealers, auction results and the dates of collectors' fairs. Further information can be found on the following websites:

Diecast Collector (UK) www.diecast-collector.com
Model Collector (UK) www.modelcollector.co.uk
Model Auto Review (UK) www.zeteo.com
Passion 43ème (France) www.passion-43.com
MiniAuto (Spain) www.revistasprofesionales.com
Auto in Miniatuur (Holland) www.namac.nl
Quattroruotine (Italy) www.quattroruote.it/modellismo
Modell Fahrzeug (Germany) www.modellfahrzeug.de

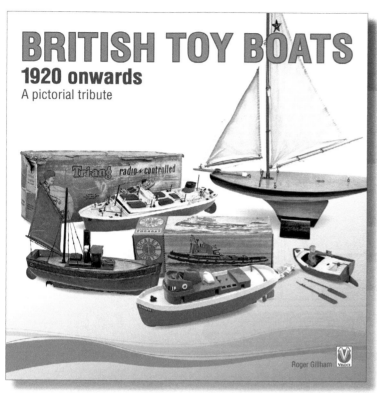
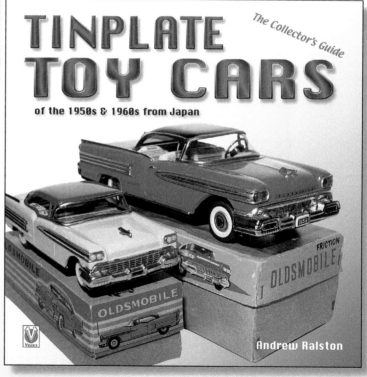

Also from Veloce Publishing –

Britains Toy Models Catalogues 1970 to 1979
with comprehensive indices

Compiled by **David Pullen**

Britains has been a world-leading toy and model manufacturer for nearly 120 years.
This book provides reprints of the annual toy models consumer catalogues issued
by Britains in the 1970s. It also contains two indices listing all the items shown in the
catalogues, complete with the original UK retail prices.
This is a beautifully illustrated, essential guide to the models Britains produced in the
1970s.

ISBN: 978-1-845842-75-8
Paperback • 14.8x21cm • 304 pages • 261 colour pictures

For more information and price details, visit our website at www.veloce.co.uk
• email: info@veloce.co.uk • Tel: +44(0)1305 260068

www.veloce.co.uk

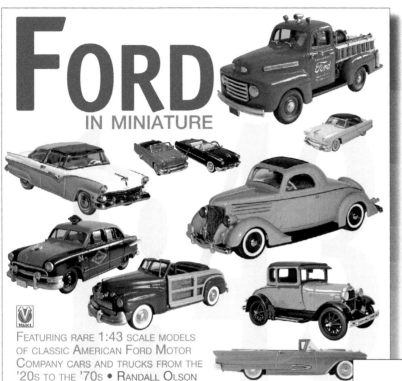

This colourful book showcases some of the most beautiful and rare scale models ever made of American Ford, Edsel, Lincoln, and Mercury cars and light trucks from the classic 1930-69 period. These unusual and expensive models have a flawless finish and astounding detail: a MUST for scale model and Ford buffs.

Paperback • 25x25cm • £19.99*
• 128 pages • 400 colour photos
• ISBN: 978-1-845840-27-3

Over 540 colour photographs of 1:43 scale model Cadillac, Chevrolet, Buick, Oldsmobile, Pontiac, and GM light trucks & cars, plus historical and technical information, comprehensive lists of models, manufacturers and builders, pricing and sources, make this book a MUST for serious GM fans and scale model collectors.

Paperback • 25x25cm • £24.99*
• 160 pages • 545 colour photos
• ISBN: 978-1-845841-56-0

INDEX